T0373375

The World Looks Like
This From Here

The World Looks Like This From Here

Thoughts on African Psychology

Kopano Ratele

WITS UNIVERSITY PRESS

Published in South Africa by:
Wits University Press
1 Jan Smuts Avenue
Johannesburg 2001

www.witspress.co.za

First published 2019

http://dx.doi.org.10.18772/12019093900

978-1-77614-390-0 (Paperback)
978-1-77614-391-7 (Web PDF)
978-1-77614-392-4 (EPUB)
978-1-77614-393-1 (Mobi)

Project manager: Lisa Compton
Copyeditor: Karen Press
Proofreader: Lee Smith
Indexer: Sanet le Roux
Cover design: Hybrid Creative
Typesetter: MPS
Typeset in 10.5 point Crimson

Contents

CONTENTS

CONTENTS

Author's note

A decade ago I would not have advised anyone to study psychology. Psychology, I would have said, is bad for your mental health, and were it to turn out that being a psychologist is good for your economic status, the likelihood is that you would be supporting the marginalisation of people who most need psychological help.

Today, I have reassessed my attitude towards psychology. Today, if a student is adamant that he wants to study psychology, having made him aware of the discipline's history and contemporary complicity with coloniality, racism, apartheid and Euroamerican-centricity, and having made sure he understands how many psychologists tend to remain silent in the face of psychological torture and oppression, I will not say, do not study psychology. I will say, do not forget to study how psychology studies people. Do not forget your self. Do not forget the people who need your help but cannot afford the ridiculous fees. Reach beyond what psychology teaches you about healing, for only then will you be able to recognise that the psychological healers themselves, especially those whose colonial and apartheid wounding has not received any attention, need healing. Reach beyond how this field in which you want expertise wants you to study humans, wants you to act towards people, other animals, plants, other living beings and the universe. Study beyond its methods, interpretations, theories and conclusions. Pay attention to its assumptions and do not get entrapped by them: to the way those who call themselves psychologists approach people and the world around them; to how those who call themselves psychotherapists go about trying to heal people and themselves. Most of all, don't be satisfied with American psychology in Africa; search for Africa in psychological theories, build a cultural home for Africans in psychology, which is to say, build a psychology that centres Africa, a conscious, critical, reflective African psychology.

Do not believe anyone who seeks to dismiss your search for a psychology that centres your experience, your knowledge, your cultural connectedness, your being as a person living in an African country.

The idea of African psychology appears to be a simple and straightforward matter. Except that it often is not. The latter situation, where there is confusion more than clarity, is usually the state of affairs.

So here it is: African psychology is not something outside of global psychology. But it goes beyond it.

African psychology is not ethnopsychology. It is not a psychology practised only on Africans, not only a psychology by African psychologists, not only for Africans. Not in my book.

African psychology is not a branch of psychology in the way cognitive psychology is.

African psychology is an integral part of all human psychology. We may even say African psychology is at the beginning of the evolution of human psychology – I am referring not to psychology as a discipline but to the way the human psyche has evolved. But that is not a central argument in this book.

This is a book about one thing, although I hope you will be able to find many useful things in it. That one thing is that African psychology is a way of looking. An orientation. A situatedness in psychology, in African societies and in the world at large. African psychology is a psychology for Africa and Africans that does not exoticise, that disalienates even while centring itself in the world. What I seek to convey in the book is the idea that to be authentic and have a meaningful life as a student of psychology in Africa, a counsellor, or a teacher of psychology, and still be at home in Africa – not only because you may be made to lose the original language of your dreams – you will have to always remind yourself to see with your own eyes, remind yourself that you are entitled to being in the world. That way of looking and seeing and acting comes from challenging the Euroamerican traditions, concepts, approaches and findings that engulf psychology in Africa, into which we, in Africa, are hailed as psychology students, teachers, therapists and researchers.

*   *   *

Many people have contributed to this book in overt and indirect, seen and indiscernible ways. Life has never been the same since I met the once most famous person in Nate Holland's universe, Ketso Ratele. Dab. I wish to make a note of my appreciation for learning from all of my PhD students in the Transdisciplinary African Psychologies Programme and the Research Unit on Men and Masculinities at the University of South Africa (Unisa), and for all the formal and informal conversations that have contributed to my ongoing thinking on African psychology. For her skill in convening the colloquia series on African psychology, belief in what we are doing, reverse management and overall doggedness, I want to thank Neziswa Titi. Rebecca Helman is not only great as an editor but also as a social advocate, a terrific student, and an enviable collaborator. Thank you for editing the first draft of the manuscript. The conversations, some very long and others in the corridors between our offices, with Refiloe Makama, Nicholas Malherbe, Sarah Day, Zenzile Molo, Josephine Cornell and Sipho Dlamini have urged me to elaborate my thoughts about African psychology. Much of Section 15 was first published as a post on 4 February 2016, in the blog *African Psychology* (https://africanpsychology.net/2016/02/04/stop-wasting-time-on-academic-fads-like-postmodern-psychology-and-build-a-world-centred-african-psychology/).

In 2016 the folk at the Psychology Department at Rhodes University invited me for a visit and I had the first opportunity to air some of the elements of my orientations framework. I want to thank them for this opportunity. The executive director and president of the Psychological Society of South Africa offered me a space in 2017 and 2018 to test some of my ideas at the Annual Congresses of Psychology and I would like to extend my appreciation. André Keet invited me to Nelson Mandela University in 2018, where I had a pleasurable interaction with psychology students: thank you brother. I am appreciative of the financial support for the book provided by the Unisa Institute for Social & Health Sciences (ISHS). I thank Monique Huysamen and Peace Kiguwa for their openness to my invitation to respond to my readings of their work.

I am fortunate to have the kind of colleagues I have in the ISHS, as well as in the South African Medical Research Council–Unisa Violence, Injury and Peace Research Unit, and I thank you all for nourishing the space we have created for each other and for our students. In particular, I am indebted to Mildred Dreyer, Samed Bulbulia, Royal Tlale Lekoba, Mohamed Seedat, Jeminah Mtshali, Luanne Swart, Anthony Phaahlamohlaka, Naiema Taliep, Tumelo Mashaba, Annelise Krige, Shahnaaz Suffla and Ashley van Niekerk.

My acknowledgement goes also to the reviewers of the manuscript of this book, who were robust in their criticisms and generous in their comments. I have been terribly impressed, at times frustrated, but could not have been given a better editor than Karen Press, who was a great writer's reader, facilitative and questioning and thorough. Roshan Cader and the folk at Wits Press are simply outstanding. Thank you very much.

And in the end, to my friend and companion, Carmine Rustin, as always, my endless gratitude and love.

1 | (African)

African, in African psychology, is tacit. It is a bracketed word. And, needless to say, African in African psychology contains the term 'Africa'. African, then, signifies both people and place – it indicates someone or something originating in or connected to a place in Africa.

2 | The necessary adjective

Confusion is never far off regarding what precisely is being referred to whenever the term 'African psychology' is uttered. We ought to note, therefore, at this early point that there is more than one way of defining African psychology. This is how my co-authors and I have written about the multiple meanings of the term: 'African psychology means the same thing as, for example, psychology *in*, *by*, *from*, or *of* Africa or Africans' (Ratele et al. 2018: 332). (I should add: psychology *for* Africa or Africans.) That is to say, African psychology can mean psychology in Western Sahara or South Sudan. It can mean psychology practised by Egyptians or Ethiopians. Psychology from Senegal or South Africa. Psychology of Africa, or of one or other African nation. Psychology for Africans. All of this implies that we always have to ask what preposition is being elided between 'psychology' and 'Africa/n', in order to define the kind of African psychology to which we are referring. It also means that there is always a question of why there should be a need for African psychology, when the *'science'* of psychology is said to be universal. But, fundamentally, it is the notion of universal human science – of its truthfulness and completeness – that is at stake: a human science that bears no marks of the humans who produce it, that has been shorn of values and normativity.

It is of utmost importance to note, then, that it is not in all of African psychology that Africa and Africans are implied – only in the kind of African psychology that will be advanced here. This is African psychology *sensu stricto* (in the narrow sense): psychology that places Africa and Africans at its centre, while simultaneously being open and talking to a wider world.

The psychology that tacitly places Africa and Africans at its centre is, however, the ideal. That psychology emerges from under the rubble of colonial ruins, apartheid racism and post-independence despotism. The time when a psychology student at the University of Johannesburg says, 'I am studying psychology,' and is immediately presumed to be referring to African psychology, is in the future. The time when a clinical psychologist working in Lagos presents a successful case using her therapeutic modality and her audience immediately grasps that she is talking of African-centred psychotherapy is yet to come. Today, to be clearly understood, we are still compelled to say African psychology. We are thus also obliged to say *African* in African psychology *must* be made tacit. We live in the age of American psychology – the psychology of the United States of America (US) – and to a lesser extent Western European psychology, taken as universal psychology. And a consequence of the hegemony of American and Western European psychology is that psychology produced outside those regions of the world, and fully conscious of its situatedness in the places where it is practised, requires an adjective in order to be granted recognition.

3 | Disorientation

What is the problem to which such a situated psychology responds? Let us call it the problem of disorientation. Or of inferiority complex. Of an upside-down world, to borrow Pal Ahluwalia's (2003: 343–345) words. Confusion. Alienation. A sense that life is always happening elsewhere.

This is the problem of the domination of a psychology made in America or Western Europe over Africa and Africans – let us simply call this psychology, whenever we can, Euroamerican or Western psychology. It is the problem of a psychology practised in Africa that has very little to say about the causes of mental illness, social pathologies, violence in its bodily, institutional, cultural, governmental, economic and political forms. It is that curious feeling you have, as an African, that the psychological explanations for what is happening to you are to be found elsewhere, not around you or in yourself. In fact, that the questions with which psychologists and psychology students ought to occupy themselves are not to be found in themselves, their families, their schools, in the relationships they have or do not have, in their neighbourhoods and workplaces, in the economies of their countries or their politics. The feeling that the questions themselves, and not only the answers, lie somewhere across the seas. And that the theories and models presented in books and journal articles published in the US and Western Europe have the solutions to that disorientation, inferiority complex, sense of living in an upside-down world, confusion, alienation – rather than being their causes.

The problem to which such a situated psychology responds, then, is the problem of living well psychologically, culturally, and not just physically, but also of dying well (in contrast to dying from preventable causes like hunger, HIV/Aids, interpersonal violence, suicide, or transport-related accidents which kill so many people in African countries).

4 | Awake to Africa

Whereas Africa tends in large measure to be regarded in psychological studies as little more than an extractive data site, to begin by thinking of Africa and African as unspoken terms in African psychology is to awake to Africa – to the fact of being African, or of researching, teaching, doing psychotherapy, or studying in a place in Africa – as ontologically and epistemologically productive elements of the process of understanding, in psychological terms, the lives of individuals in the countries of Africa, from Algeria to Zimbabwe.

To be able to fully realise such a situated psychology, one that authoritatively but wordlessly situates Africa and the dynamic and complex psychological lives of Africans – the cognitive, emotional, motivational, relational, experiential, cultural and behavioural aspects of their lives – at the centre of the field of psychology, is the ultimate epistemic (regarding questions of knowledge) and ontological (concerned with questions of what it means to be human and to live with other forms of life) goal of this kind of African psychology. What is that African psychology to which we are referring, after all, if not a situated psychology?

At the same time, because African psychology demands engagement in what the black Caribbean Africana philosopher Lewis Gordon (2007: 121) calls 'explicit adjectival techniques of appearance', consciously centring Africa and Africans in psychology, as in all of the sciences and the arts, *without uttering* these terms, is something we must learn to do. To do African psychology without explicitly mentioning Africa is to clear space in the present and in history, and prevail over the erasures of Euroamerican psychology. To do psychology that

assumes Africa is to claim recognition and, even more critically, to assert the fact that all of the world can be cognised
from here. Because, on the whole, only a psychology that
centres on a certain life lived in Western Europe and the US
has so far enjoyed the power of referring to itself without the
need for adjectives, and doing African psychology can mean
feeling compelled to locate your work as African. The goal is
to make this unnecessary, although the compulsion imposed
by Euroamerican psychologists, journal editors and reviewers,
and book publishers is quite real. With the turn to the right in
political and social Europe, maybe even in the psychologies of
Europeans after the decision by the United Kingdom to leave
the European Union (EU), with the embarrassment brought
about by the election of Donald Trump as president of the US
after the false promise of a post-racial world that was meant
to be ushered in by Barack Obama, with the economic rise of
China, the centre has decisively shifted and the world will keep
changing. In the case of China's ambitions in Africa and with
its Belt and Road Initiative, the world seems to be opening up,
while in other cases new borders are being raised; these open-
ings, closures and shifts ought to be evaluated for the future
possibilities, potential networks and new work opportunities
they create for African scholars in psychology. A space to assert
different perspectives, divergent knowledges and other ways of
being in the world seems to have become possible. Hence, the
goal of doing African psychology without a sense of inferiority
has come closer to being realised.

5 | A way of seeing

Although this is neither always nor fully appreciated, African in African psychology is best when unexpressed. At its strongest point, like a deeply held belief, African in African psychology is *the presumed*. A way of seeing. A way grounded in, for instance, the sense of hearing, thus listening and speaking and ultimately language – a key subject in cultural debates on the effects of colonialism on African intellectual thought, but also in African psychology when it comes to the question of whether we can fully understand and heal people's emotional and mental pain if we do not understand the language in which they are most at home. A way grounded in the sense of touch and its situated meanings; taste and its literal and figurative denotations and connotations; and smell and its associations, including the smells of food, in the air, about places, of bodies, smells that attract or repel us just outside of our conscious awareness.

This claim is founded on the understanding that there are no value-neutral ways of seeing, feeling or thinking. None is unaffected by power. Certainly, there are no value-barren modes of being, no forms of existence outside the reach of what is desirable, good, right, worthy or valued – and of their opposites. African in African psychology is, therefore, an enunciation. A situated practice. A wordless act involving the whole of your being. It articulates and enacts your position in the world. It is an act that reads, *the world looks like this from here.*

Here, to be clear, is not just a place. Here is more than simply the place where the body stands looking, the eyes in the head that look out. The self itself is here. Here refers to the self that is inside, and extends (from) the body. You say, telling the other over the phone, *I* am *here*. What do you mean? Are you only saying that your body is sitting in a chair in a coffee shop, in a town, in a certain country, in the world? Ultimately you want it to be understood that *you*, all of your *self*, is here. Here, then, is the self that looks. We look with the whole of our selves.

It is true, though, that among those who have lived below the line that separates humans from the three-fifths beings (enslaved humans who perforce cannot self-determine, and do not have the same rights as free humans; in slavocratic America, an enslaved black, seen as not-fully-human, was counted as three-fifths of a free person), those whose languages have died or are dying, whose names have been taken away from them, whose minds have been used against them, whose bodies have been used to enrich others, it is common to find a schoolchild who is alienated from speaking in her mother tongue, from seeing with her own eyes, or from expressing her feelings. Where this alienation from ourselves, from our thoughts, views, words or emotions, exists, what we must aim for is nothing less than self-emancipation. We must strive for psychological self-determination, mental freedom, emotional autonomy, spiritual liberation and cultural rights just as much as for socioeconomic rights and political independence. We must 'decolonise the mind', to use the injunction famously associated with Kenyan novelist and essayist Ngũgĩ wa Thiong'o (1986).

Alienation divides me from you, you from her, her from others. It recreates the lack inside yourself. But it does more than just divide you from others. The division that alienates one person from another can have any basis: your nationality, the school you went to, how much money you have, the neighbourhood in which you live, your sexual choices, the theories you use to explain things, the languages you speak, whether you speak with an 'accent', the labels you wear. The division may be accidental, but its effects are calculated. Nothing is beyond use by the forces that seek to isolate us from each other. Anything can be employed to oppress us, to numb our empathy with others, to rupture our human solidarity with others.

Colonialism and racial apartheid were centred on the body, which is a way of saying that they racialised us. Racial alienation was woven into the system of economic control. The greatest achievement of those social and political forces that would alienate us from each other has been getting us to think in particular ways about our bodies, but also about our ideas, feelings and selves. Getting us to believe in the naturalness of race, and of the division of humans into racial groups.

The body from which we look at the world, at ourselves and others, is inextricably tied to our sense of the world, our sense of self and of other humans. But we are our bodies just as much as we are our minds. Therefore being black is a material-psychological state. To refer to yourself or to be referred to as black is to employ the discourse of race – that is to say, to refer to the effect of racial-ising ideological processes, processes that are not simply about recognising how people look different in terms of skin colour but are used to shape the cultural, political and economic order.

Racialisation involves categorising humans socially on the basis of their phenotypical features – how they look to the outside observer. Race is not something that sprang up of its own accord, outside of how the world is thought of or socially constituted by humans. There would be no need for racialisation if not for racism, in fact. It is not racism that is derived from a scientific process of classifying humans. The very process of allocating people to something called race groups is derived from racist consciousness. The categorisation of humans into race groups emanates from a colonial racist project – the project to dominate those who are to be regarded as Other, to sell them, and to exploit their bodies and labour. Being black is a consequence of such racial categorisation – to be exact, a consequence of the ideology of racial superiority and inferiority, a way in which some people come to be seen and to see themselves in many countries where race is central to the political and economic order. And, due to the globalisation of racism and its attendant idea of racial classes, there are few if any places in the world where these racialising processes are unknown; they are at work even in countries like Iceland, Japan and Kyrgyzstan which are more homogeneous, and where race may not be a legislated or politically sanctioned way in which people identify themselves. To walk while being black in a world constituted by colonial and contemporary global racism involves the body, but of course also the psyche – or more precisely, consciousness – and the Others, those who are seen as essentially different from the self and yet, because of this difference, constitutive of the black self. It incorporates the sensations on the skin, the thoughts in the brain, affect (observable emotions, including mood) and momentary and more durable interpersonal relations. It is in the company of Others, especially, that the self experiences this race-fullness, as opposed to what might be referred to as simply being human, that is to say, being unraced – experiencing the world as if there were no races, only people.

We know that to walk while black – or to look, hang around, earn a living while black; to love, speak, or let others know you are in pain – is potentially dangerous for the self. We must therefore underline that there is positive affect to be experienced once having got to understand how we become black, and hence well-being in talking and walking black, loving black, looking black and being black. A world of difference exists between regarding being black as a source of connectedness, happiness and pride, and seeing it as a devalued and loveless negative identity.

Racialising processes are applicable to white people too, of course. In whiteness-dominated societies, the racial order privileges those who are regarded as white over those categorised as black; the consequences of these two processes are different. All the same, being white, just like being black, is not only a question of an individual identity and an economic position, but also a material-psychological state.

Colonialism, which is inextricably tied to slavery and anti-black racism, has arranged bodies into hierarchies of value so as to cut us apart from each other. As the original apartheid, colonialism had violence of difference types and the threat of violence as key mechanisms. Similar violence was evident in chattel slavery. And violence, sometimes physical as in cases where black men get killed or profiled by the police in the US and in South Africa, at other times indirect, structural or psychological, is a characteristic of contemporary global racism. In this way, to speak of colonialism is to bring people to awareness of what is oppressing them and others. Colonialism, in varied ways, was interested in what the black body and the mind of the 'native' (who was the Other, defined and fixed in opposition to the white, European coloniser) did and could be made to endure, under pain of violence. It found expression in the very idea that there are some groups of people who have the right to control others, to determine what work they are permitted to do, who among them has the right to be a citizen, how far they can be educated, where they may live, whom they may have sex with. At the same time, the colonial powers of Europe were applying these lessons about violence and how to control human beings in the colonies to the populations of their own metropoles. Indeed, scholars have argued that the genocide perpetrated during the Second World War was first tested by the German colonisers among the Herero of Namibia in 1904 (Adhikari 2008; Gewald 2003; Melber 2005).

And so you have to learn, then, how to see yourself clearly again. How to be whole again. Through this process of understanding colonial alienation you learn to relate again to your body and mind and affect, as well as to others, with authenticity. You are re-educated to become conscious about where you are standing when you look at yourself and at others, when you read journal articles and books, when you watch television, plays and films, or interpret people's behaviour.

For now, though, in order to show why *this* – the imperative to see from Africa, to look with our whole selves from here, ultimately to reconfigure how we do psychology in Africa – has to be so, we have to *speak* African psychology.

African in African-centred psychology is a way of being in the world. African-centred psychology seeks to generate and inculcate ways of seeing, of feeling, of thinking and of doing. It is for this reason that it will have achieved its greatest expression, its most vital ends, when the term 'African' in the phrase 'African-centred psychology' is no longer necessary. When the self and the work of psychology are situated in this way, Africa must be considered a term in brackets. You no longer have to say, I am situating myself in an African-centred way. You *just do it*: you situate yourself at the centre.

You begin by learning how you have been situating yourself, how you have been situated. With deliberation you move from the margins to the centre. You acquire the habit of seeing from Africa. However, to get to that point where Africa is the unexpressed figure in African-centred psychology, you must utter the term 'African'. Until we arrive at the point where Africa has become our default perspective, we are compelled to write it (without brackets).

6 | Off-centre

It is necessary to underline this distinction: not all African psychology is necessarily Africa-centred. This is a key idea. A difference ought to be recognised between those positions in psychology that centre Africa, that take Africa as a place from which one sees, from where the voice projects, and those that apprehend Africa as one among several sites of investigation or as a site of application. This differentiation between psychology that uses Africa as a site of data collection or application and psychology that regards Africa as a place of theory production is as vital as the idea of plurality within the body of work referred to as African psychology; it underscores the idea of African psychology as a set of orientations and not as itself a sub-discipline, or an applied branch of globalised – we will not be wrong to say world-colonising – Western-centric psychology like neuropsychology, health psychology, or human development.

It is not uncommon for African psychologists in their classes and consulting rooms to teach or work with disaffecting notions, models, approaches and texts that misrecognise a myriad of African experiences. Carrying in our brains at least two unequal and often enough antagonistic cultures, many of us offer therapy or teach in an 'upside-down world', the words Pal Ahluwalia used when discussing Frantz Fanon's nausea brought on by his confrontation with a white child and its mother on a street in France, which was to bring Fanon the insight that he was hated, and that the world was not what he had been made to think it was: he was not a Frenchman but a 'body in the third person' (Ahluwalia 2003: 344). The world of African psychologists is a world in which Africa itself is off-centre, blurry, even pathologised. To speak of an upside-down world replete with misrecognition is to attempt to bring to awareness the position from which we see the world and, of course, from which the world sees us: the terms of our meeting with other humans and animals and the natural environment, our engagement with texts, our transactions with institutions, and our negotiations with the larger world in which we exist. What troubles us, then, is a sense of dislocation, of life lived in multiple time zones, of blurred perspectives, of disrupted flows of consciousness. For those who would teach, or offer explanations, or seek to heal disorders, this sense of living with interrupted and multiple temporalities raises questions of centres and margins, of imposed explanations as opposed to an understanding of subjects in their striving, and just as often, questions of failure to fathom the labyrinth of a meaningful life among the people we seek to heal and teach.

7 | Words are not enough

A basic idea, and yet so consequential: the term 'African' in African psychology achieves its highest aim if it has sunk into the depths of the speaking subject's subconscious. I do not have to say, this is my way of seeing the world. Seeing the world from *here* has become a subconscious habit through a paradoxical process of consciousness-raising.

Rarely are words ever enough; I am painfully aware of this. It is perhaps unsatisfactory to simply tell you that African in African psychology is most powerful when it reaches the level of the taken-for-granted; when we have managed, as individuals or groups, to forget what we were taught to see. People quite often forget who they are, and poetic, enchanting, musical words are seldom all they need. Is it not obvious, then, what is required? We must build shiny modern monuments to the gods of African-centredness. Create university departments and research centres where developing 'ways of seeing from Africa' is a core value and mission. And why not entire universities? Erect graceful temples, great and small, to the idea. Make objects sculptural, visual and tactile in a multitude of forms and shapes which express the idea of a world centred in Africa in so many diverse ways. Produce different tools, tests and techniques. That is what we ought to do.

8 | Teaching Africa

They are not many fathers who teach their children that they are African, and what that fully entails; that is to say, teach the child directly about what living as an African is, or is not, and what it can be. It is true, though, that some of them are raised hearing from adults around them what the Sesotho word *botho* means – that is, what being human entails, as they learn how to behave towards others, how to think of themselves as members of a community of individuals who respect and take care of each other – and what it is not. But how many parents do actually teach their children directly about being African? For that matter, who has received direct and comprehensive instruction in what it means to be black? Not many, not directly, and not in any classroom in the course of their basic schooling or university education.

The first lesson involved in teaching African psychology is thus to teach Africa. Perhaps all courses about African psychology are essentially directed at learning and teaching about Africa in the world. The world from Africa. And yet, once again, the best of African psychology courses are those that can manage to teach Africa and being African in the world well, without mentioning the words 'Africa' and 'African'.

I suspect that not many normal white parents, in Africa, America, Europe or elsewhere, teach their children that they are white. By normal, I mean those individuals who do not consider themselves racist. I do not suppose they tell their children to enjoy their white privilege.

This is what puts me in mind to ask, in the context of working to realise African-centred psychology: what do we teach the young and each other about being African in today's world? How can we not teach Africa in psychology, in today's world? Given Africa's economic position relative to North America, Western Europe, Australia and China, the assumption I make is that it is a virtuous thing to teach Africa, to learn about being African in the world, so as to withstand the arrows of global apartheid and racism, and the subtle and overt valuing of whiteness or the privileges that come with a US or EU passport when compared to African ones. And since it is inadequate to ask only about why to teach Africa and what to teach, we also must ask, when is the optimal period to teach about being African? During the first year of undergraduate study? The final year? In pre-university education?

The same applies to black parents and lessons on blackness, in Africa or elsewhere: is it still a good thing to teach black children about being black? In light of the persistence of racism – which lies at the root of the white saviour dream, the dreamlike belief of colonists about the Dark Continent, the American dream, the white South African dream – I presume it remains a virtue to teach about the slings, sorrows, resilience and triumphs of black people in a world in which they were dehumanised. Are dehumanised. Again, the question is, in today's world, in this place, what to teach about being black, when to teach it, and how?

These are matters with which we have to come to grips if we are to make African-centred psychology real. To do African-centred work is to raise consciousness, or more precisely, to engage in what the Brazilian philosopher of education and advocate of anti-oppressive pedagogy Paulo Freire (2005) referred to as conscientisation (a matter to which we shall return).

9 | Psychology is culture

Harry Charalambos Triandis was born in 1926 in Greece. In his twenties he left his ancestral home for Canada, where he did his undergraduate studies at McGill University. He moved on to the University of Toronto for further studies before going down to Cornell University in the US for his doctoral work. Triandis is important here not because he went on to occupy several noteworthy positions in the American and international psychology fraternity, including serving as president of the International Association of Cross-Cultural Psychology. His importance stems from the fact that in one of his books he actually mentions Africa. It is not a flattering mention. This does not mean that those who do not mention Africa do not hold views about it; but, having had the courage to utter the word, Triandis offers us something to which we can directly respond. In the book in question, *Culture and Social Behaviour*, published in 1994, this Greek-born and Western-educated social psychologist relates an interesting story about the first time he visited India in 1965. It is a tale about a hotel in Mysore, recounting an inconvenience caused by an amusing cultural misunderstanding and an ensuing happy ending. The point of the story is that 'we are not aware of our own culture unless we come in contact with another one' (Triandis 1994: 3). After narrating the anecdote, Triandis writes:

> While this anecdote is amusing and instructive, it raises an important issue: how much of the context of psychology may in fact be a distortion when applied to other cultures? When I started editing the six-volume *Handbook of Cross-Cultural Psychology*, I asked myself that question. I wrote to some forty colleagues, all over

the world, and asked them to send me psychological findings from their culture that are not totally in agreement with findings published in the West. I got back very little. I was frustrated until Terry Prothro, then at the American University in Beirut, Lebanon, pointed out to me that our *training and methods* are also culture bound, and it is difficult to find new ideas without the theoretical and methodological tools that can extract them from a culture. Most of the people I had written to had gotten their doctorates in Western universities and would not have been especially good at analyzing their own cultures from a non-Western viewpoint. Examining one's own culture takes special effort. It is only in the last thirty-five years or so that systematic attempts have been made to analyse social behaviour cross-culturally. (1994: 3; emphasis mine)

I wish to add that it takes not just special individual effort but specialised training, too, for us to see our own culture, let alone others' cultures in their fullness.

I suspect there are a number of culturally intelligent African, US and Western European psychologists. But presumably Triandis did not know many such culturally astute researchers from Africa, Asia, or Latin America. He did say that most of the people he had written to had studied in the West. They were Westernised. But a critical set of epistemological weaknesses lies in assuming that the best analysts of a culture are those educated at universities, and that psychologists are best placed to do cultural or cross-cultural analysis. These assumptions can blind us to some of the best cultural analyses that the world offers. They are assumptions that convey a certain restricted view about knowledge.

Triandis also says some other things that are worth taking note of. The first is that cultural psychological analysis does not simply bubble up to consciousness because you are born in a culture. It takes learning to examine and understand your own culture, and the culture of others. What Triandis does not say is this: psychology is culture. It does not stand outside of culture. To study psychology is to study culture. What happens, then, if the culture in which students study psychology is not the same as the culture in which the psychology they study was born and nourished? That is to say, could there be places in the world where to study psychology is not to study culture? The answer, I am afraid, is yes.

The second thing Triandis points out, though not strongly enough, is that culture is not only about values (or beliefs, or some other necessary but soft and invisible phenomenon). Culture is about practice. Training is a cultural *practice*. Learning is cultural *practice*. We are trained into a cultural way of *doing* and *speaking* and *feeling* and *dreaming* and *thinking* and *relating* and *seeing*. In this view, the training of clinical psychologists is cultural training. The same holds true for neuropsychologists, social psychologists, feminist psychoanalysts, or any other type of psychologist.

In a similar sense, methods are cultural technologies. Research methods, for instance, by which are meant systematised ways of investigating phenomena, are made possible by how members of a culture think, feel and act. Research methods are a culturally legitimated way of creating and ascertaining what counts as true knowledge. As such, methods, whether they are to do with research or with therapy, are embedded in culture, and culture is embedded in methods. Methods make possible certain culturally acceptable, sanctioned knowledge or modes of healing, and occlude other kinds of knowledge and healing.

I was most interested – and most displeased – not by Triandis's amusing anecdote and what is instructive about it in relation to psychology, but by something else he says on the following page. He writes that although there has been an increase in efforts to understand the cross-cultural aspects of social behaviour,

> [t]here are barriers to such understanding. During my travels to Africa, Asia, and Latin America, I met many psychologists and was especially impressed by the fact that many of them have *an inferiority complex*. The West is the standard, especially in psychology. Many of these psychologists assume that if their data do not match the Western theories, something is wrong with the data, not the theories. (1994: 4; emphasis mine)

What Triandis says is not totally false. His remark has a direct bearing on the endeavour to nurture and raise high African-centred psychological theories, methods, courses, and therapies and investigations. When will we be done with these pervasive, debilitating inferiority complexes?

10 | Africa internationalised

Some gains for African-centred psychological work will issue from publishing internationally. There is little doubt about this. African-centred psychology must internationalise if it is to influence the world. If we do not universalise we shall not avoid ghettoisation.

I should be clearer. Of course it is always a little hard to persuade editors of 'international' journals – which is how journals published in the US and Western Europe are referred to in my country – and reviewers in other countries of the solidity and quality of your work, especially if such work goes against the orthodoxy of the discipline. The effort of persuasion is harder for some than for others. It is easier for those who are happy to go along with the globally hegemonic forms of knowledge, methods and tools of analysis, and harder for those who refuse to succumb to the orthodoxy. The latter is the case when it comes to African-centred work that fundamentally challenges how the world is ordered and perceived. In such cases, you have to sweat to convince editors and reviewers that Africa is a place of *making thought*. You are more than likely to have to work very hard to convince others that Africa is not only a site of data collection, but one where explanations and concepts – what is often pretentiously called Theory – are generated that are as valid as those from anywhere else in the world. It can be tiresome to put effort into trying to convince people that you, as a professional psychologist, have original thoughts, let alone that a ninety-year-old man who grows his own vegetables, raises his grandchildren, draws a government pension, but has never actually published an article, has a considered psychological perspective which should receive equal due to that of a psychology professor. Some will die spiritually or culturally – have died – trying to show some famous name who knows nothing about Africa and his students that African perspectives, conceptualisations and explanations matter.

But, again, there are some gains to be made, no doubt, from working to publish African-centred psychological research and theory with international publishers and in international journals. And even if what you publish will matter to only a couple of open-minded scholars and students, not to most US or European psychologists or their students, it is always worthwhile to realise that it is a hard climb to get to the top, wherever that is. To get used to the knowledge that the rules are not in your favour, if you write from Africa and want more than to be a mere mimic. To get used to the fact that you will face tremendous barriers if you refuse to 'go along to get along'. But also to recognise that there are people in the US or Western Europe who critically appreciate the consequences of the global economy of knowledge dominated by the West.

That being the case, the greatest African-centred psychological work will come from learning not to give a fuck, deep down, about what reviewers, journal editors, or universities that want you to publish in so-called international journals think. You don't have to curse. But you should not give 'international' journals, reviewers and editors so much power over you. The same goes for established researchers and academics within your country. They will tell you that you do not know what you are on about. They will want you to change how you think about your subject. You have to recognise this and understand what it signifies. That's where you begin. *Here* is where you begin. That is to say, here matters, your consciousness matters. Your voice matters. This is always what it is about: your home, your words, your point of view, your consciousness, how they matter, to whom, and to what end.

Consider this: if you do not think and feel and behave as if where and how you live matter, why should others think and feel that you matter? If you are not convinced that where and how you were raised, what and how you think, what you see and how you see the world matter, who will be convinced? Of course, you have to realise that your thoughts or feelings or actions might not matter so much to others – not as much as their lives matter to them – unless what you do injures or interferes with them. Reconcile yourself to this fact at the earliest opportunity, that opportunity being now. As a student and a young scholar, you will have to recognise that what you think and see and do really does not matter as much to other people – in particular those in the well-funded universities, departments and research centres – as it does to you. As such, what you need to learn is not to give a toss about this, and to free yourself to do meaningful work. If you cannot do work that has meaning for you, you can try instead to do important, useful, or really interesting work.

11 | Aiming for redundancy

It is no exaggeration to say that such a simple conception of African-centred psychology – that the term 'African' in African-centred psychology attains its key objective if it has become redundant – is perhaps the most important idea a psychology student, teacher or researcher will come to hold. Along with the idea of African-centred psychology as a way of seeing from somewhere, it is certainly the single most significant idea about psychology I have arrived at since I began my career as a university teacher and researcher.

In comparison to psychologists, philosophers are often keener to trouble how we think through such a thing as 'thinking from Africa'. You do not necessarily have to plough through Kwame Appiah, Angela Davis, Cheikh Anta Diop, Emmanuel Chukwudi Eze, Paulin Hountondji, Adrian Piper, Léopold Senghor, Cornel West, Kwasi Wiredu and the many other philosophers who have arrived at this reference-frame-altering notion. (Of course, you can also seek help in the works of well-known names – Hannah Arendt, Aristotle, Judith Butler, Hélène Cixous, Jacques Derrida, Rene Descartes, Michel Foucault, Plato, or Jean-Paul Sartre – but my suspicion is that they will not have a ready answer for you.) I propose that a simple but consciousness-shifting insight such as this is not to be found in any of the abstruse philosophy books you might read. Coming to consciousness about Africa in psychology, as distinct from psychology in Africa, needs more than reading. It is of some help to read, do not misconstrue me. Writing and reading form a kind of discussion, certainly. That is why I have set time aside to put together this slim volume of thoughts: so that it can be read. Perhaps, in the age of Facebook, you will 'like' it. But I would be most satisfied if I were to be challenged about this conception.

A fuller understanding of, say, the (African) psychology of men's aggression – that is to say, of the psychology of men as always a psychology *from* a place of men *in* a place – demands that we do other kinds of work than simply reading Euroamerican psychological texts: legwork, searching, looking at the men with our own eyes, learning to see the world through the men's eyes, talking to one another, learning together, being open to each other's criticisms. Only out of such work comes the development of ways of seeing differently. Only through such work do we avoid oppressing while alleging that we aim to heal.

I am reminded of a question I was asked a while ago. I had been repeating a well-known fact that appears curiously neglected in all the talk about violence: that is, that in South Africa, as in Brazil and the US and several other countries, black men and other young men of colour (in which category, in this specific case, I include Hispanics in the US and those who are still referred to as coloureds in South Africa) constitute a disproportionately high number of victims of deadly violence. The question I was asked was why the burden of victimisation through fatal violence does not fall on young white men. The answer to that question has everything to do with African-centred knowledge. It runs something like this. Men who do not achieve culturally respected masculinity in their society are more likely to employ their bodies to try to reach for recognition and respect. Bodies employed in this way – as a way of proving masculinity – are more likely to be exposed to injury and death. Why is culturally respected masculinity achievable for some men and not others? It is the dominant culture, or the dominant group within the culture, that determines what kind of man deserves respect, in other words what counts as successful masculinity. In societies like South Africa, Brazil and the US, societies that have sizable black populations and that are dominated by upper-middle-class white men, upper-middle-class white patriarchal values are the standard against which all men have to measure themselves. Men from lower strata of society struggle to make the grade. Is it not obvious, then, what African-centred knowledge can do for these men? In a word, African-centred psychological knowledge is knowledge that sees the struggles for recognition as men from the perspective of the men most subject to victimisation.

12 | Overlooked perspectives

In an article with the title '"Too good to be real": The obviously augmented breast in women's narratives of cosmetic surgery', published in 2013 in the journal *Gender & Society*, Debra Gimlin writes that 'in Westernised societies, no other aspect of women's embodiment is as scrutinized or as emblematic of femininity as breasts' (2013: 918). What this otherwise interesting article appears unaware of are the complex ways in which women's breasts are perceived among groups such as young Swati and Zulu women, in eSwatini and South Africa. This complexity is tied to the idea of Westernisation. It may well be true that women's breasts are the most scrutinised parts of their bodies in Westernised societies. At the same time, the notion of 'Westernised societies' referred to in this case is not unpacked. Is the reference to countries in the West? To predominantly white countries? If the intention was to speak about all Westernised societies, which includes not only countries of the West but all those societies which were colonised by Europe and therefore Westernised, then the author has excluded several societies, including those in Africa, in which the discourse on women's embodiment and femininity is denser precisely because of the existence of more than one competing discourse on femininity; where society does borrow the fetishising narrative of the breast from the West but there is also a destabilisation of such fetishisation because the society has other narratives. How is this critique, which simultaneously dismisses a whole part of the world, to be read then? Some of what the author notes may actually apply to how women's bodies are regarded in countries that are excluded from the 'Westernised societies' referred to. Some does not apply. And the apparent ignorance on the part of some feminist scholars about how women's bodies and femininity are perceived in Westernised African societies is yet another call to feminist and other critical African female and male scholars to 'write African femininities and masculinities' for the world. Even if it is just one among thousands of instances, does this example not indicate the persistent need to understand society, the body and the psyche from African-centred perspectives?

13 | Unselfconscious situatedness

It took my leaving teaching in a university psychology department, eleven years after I had walked into a university as a young lecturer, to arrive at this simple insight: to understand yourself as a(n) (Africa-centring) psychologist, you are compelled to work yourself towards a position where Africa is bred-in-the-bone. It can take time, in the face of received hegemonic psychology. Perhaps I am a slow learner. In total I had had the experience of nearly two decades within universities before I arrived at the full consciousness of what it means to do African-centred psychology. What it means for me to unselfconsciously situate my practice as an African at the centre of global psychology.

14 | Own goal

Of course, an African-centred psychologist can say, 'I study cognitive development from an African perspective.' But the moment you utter those words, despite your apparent aim in doing so, you have already betrayed your real intention. Your real intention is to persuade the audience of the rightness of your study. As such, you have undermined the potential influence of the study.

15 | African scholarship

More than eight years ago the Psychology Department of Rhodes University initiated an award to honour prominent members of the psychology community in South Africa for their contribution to social change in various fields of practice. The Psychology and Social Change Award is intended to

> acknowledge people who have gone beyond the traditional bounds of the discipline and contributed, through intellectual, professional and personal labour, to social change and transformation in South Africa; expose students to these kinds of role models within psychology; and to think deeply about the role of psychology in relation to facilitating as well as understanding social change. (Rhodes University 2019)

The first person to receive the award was Noel Chabani Manganyi. Aesthete, quiet yet incisive political observer, university leader, educationalist, and of course eminent psychologist, Manganyi would have been my choice, too, for an award such as this. And for many others – if we had them.

The man has had many achievements in his long life. However, it is the numerous adversities he has confronted and overcome that seem to have shaped him, as someone with an irrepressible point of view in a world that not only repressed men and women like him, but as often jailed, banned, or killed those, like him, who stood against apartheid. As for achievements in the field of psychology, Manganyi was the first to plant a seed for the growth of a psychology of black being. Over a period of just under two decades, in addition to numerous academic articles, he published his ideas in several books concerning blackness and racism. Among the works in his *oeuvre* are *Being-Black-in-the-World* (1973), *Alienation and the Body in Racist Society: A Study of the Society that Invented Soweto* (1977a), *Mashangu's Reverie, and Other Essays* (1977b), *Looking through the Keyhole: Dissenting Essays on the Black Experience* (1981) and *Treachery and Innocence: Psychology and Racial Difference in South Africa* (1991). How incredible is it that Manganyi's work does not form the core of the 'psychology of race and racism' curriculum? A southern psychology of being black, of being in the world from the perspective of South African blackness, one that can lead to a more global understanding of what it feels like to be black – what it looks like, what experience is generated by the fact of being black and living in this place at this time – is something that is still very much in need of cultivation.

Subsequent recipients of the Psychology and Social Change Award have been Dr Yogan Pillay (2009), Professor Pumla Gobodo-Madikizela (2010), Professor Hlengiwe Buhle Mkhize (2011), Professor Cheryl de la Rey (2012), Professor Melvyn Freeman (2013) and Professor Mohamed Seedat (2014). In 2015, I had the honour of following on these talented women and men in accepting the award.

The recipient of the award is asked to present a public lecture on a topic of her or his choice under the broad theme of social transformation. I elected to present a lecture on my new work on African psychology, with a specific focus on men and masculinity. It was the first time I publicly expressed in a lecture my long search for Africa in studies in the field of psychology and the interdisciplinary field of men and masculinities, as well as for how research, teaching and public intellectual work in these fields can and might contribute to studies of Africa.

16 | Education as ethical responsibility

Today, there may be a constitutional right to education in many countries in Africa. Throughout history, across Africa and in other parts of the world, men and women in church groups, political organisations, social movements, or as individuals have agitated for education. This right to education is absolutely important to treasure, especially given that there are still countries where education is not a right, or where, even though it is a right, obvious structural barriers exist that prevent some groups from gaining access to it. If you are poor, for instance, what you get may or may not be what you need or want. A great deal of what you get does not amount to much when it comes to learning how to live with self-esteem, pride, love, purpose and meaning. Poverty ought not to undermine the right to education, but where education is commoditised it does limit your educational choices as far as quality is concerned.

To overcome the effects of a dehumanising history, not merely in order to be rich but to learn to live a life full of significance, even if your parents were poor and unschooled – that's exactly what you won't get from the right to education if your teachers don't care for *the whole of you* as a person. You are more than just your brain or your body.

Even though I acknowledge the imperative of affirming education as a legal human right, I am struck by the fact that there is rarely ever an ethical obligation for those who look after the education of the young to ascertain that they are well taught. To be taught well can mean many things. To someone like me, keeping the notion of African-centredness in mind, it means that African children and young people, and all others who wish to study, are educated such that they will enjoy a meaningful life after their education. It means that they are taught how to be free, if they live in a country that has endured years of dehumanisation and oppression. It means that they learn how to live-with-others (this lesson on living-with-others being concerned with the values of *botho* referred to earlier), if their society is one in which living apart from 'others' was for a long time a way of life. Getting an education so that you can get a job is undeniably important, but a meaningless job is precisely what results when the task of educating the young is thought of only as a legalistic right, not an ethical responsibility.

It is difficult to implement the right to be taught well, of course. But it seems that, in those cases where a country has overcome colonial rule or other forms of tyranny, ignoring the question of what education is for, and how children, youth or adults who wish to learn are to be taught, leaves learners at the mercy of bad educators. It implies that you have to look elsewhere to learn the important life lessons – such as how to live an authentic life, whether there are cases where violence is justifiable, how much money it takes to be happy in our society, whether forgiveness is always good, whether monogamy is the best way to organise family relationships, why we are attracted to those who look like us in terms of their colour, whether prayer works. Is it any wonder that even in countries like South Africa where there is a constitutional right to education, too many children drop out of school?

17 | Black children and white dolls

My search for how to see from Africa, authentically, had been going on for fifteen years when I received the Psychology and Social Change Award from Rhodes University. Or at least, that's what I said to my audience when I gave my lecture at the university. But this is off by decades. The search had begun almost immediately after the first lecture I attended as a psychology student. I still remember when I learned that black children, like white children, tend to prefer white dolls. I would come to know the names of the researchers who made this discovery: the black American psychologists Kenneth Clark (1914–2005) and Mamie Clark (1917–1983). To summarise their findings in one sentence, the doll-preference studies were simply showing that black children preferred and identified with whiteness more than blackness.

In 1955 Kenneth Clark published the book *Prejudice and Your Child*. His intended audience appears to have been black (or as black Americans were referred to then, Negro) parents. Here is an extract from the book:

> In spite of the important and rapid steps toward better race relations in the larger society, the Negro parent is still faced with the responsibility of providing his children with the basic foundations of a healthy personality. It is difficult for these children to feel that they are of value unless they are given such indications within the intimate family unit. Negro children need special assurance that their parents love them and want them. These children need to know that this love is unconditional – that they are loved because they are

human beings worthy of love and respect from other human beings. Paradoxically, the social forces that necessitate this relationship in the Negro family may interfere with the ability of these parents, particularly of the working classes, to express warmth, love, and acceptance for their children – for the Negro parent is himself the product of racial pressures and frustrations. It is imperative, however, that this cycle be broken. Because it cannot be broken by the child, it must be broken by parents and by the larger society. (1955: 115)

The question I had when I came across the Clarks' original studies (Clark & Clark 1939a, 1939b, 1940, 1950) was, could this be true for South Africa? To explain my desire to find an answer to this question, I must mention that I came across the work of the Clarks while living in the midst of the cruel and dehumanising legal system of apartheid. I wanted to know: would I have chosen white dolls, if I had been in the position of those African American children? What was the difference between black children in South Africa – the country where I lived – and black children in America? There was, at the time, no scientific answer to these questions. There is still very little research in existence that could definitively answer them.

There are some problems with, and criticisms that can be made about, the Clarks' work. Some of the problems are ontological. Others epistemological. And yet others are methodological. But perhaps there are two main telling shortcomings. First, the Clarks were reformists, not radical enough. They seem to have wanted black Americans to be treated as equals in a society built on racist inequality. Their assumptions were all politically conservative.

Second, and more crucially, there are historical and contemporary continuities and convergences that have to be appreciated between blackness in America and blackness in Africa. However, there are dissimilarities that do not have to be glossed. For example, there are particular contextual meanings that US blackness has acquired, and difficulties and triumphs that black people in America have experienced, which can be contrasted to meanings of blackness in Africa and the problems and gains of black people on the continent.

Of course the work of black American psychologists is required reading for black psychology students everywhere. However, while it is essential to take cognisance of the work of African American psychologists, African psychology from Africa will not flourish if the dominance of white American psychology is merely replaced by a dominant black American psychology. Centring Africans, and specifically in this instance African children, in psychology will not develop if the universalisation of American children persists, even if those children are black. Also, it is vital to ask whether the results of research conducted in the US in the mid-twentieth century are applicable to South Africa in the twenty-first century. All the same, Kenneth Clark's assessment quoted above is one of the simplest and best conclusions about the way children learn to love, or not love, their bodies, minds and faces. A task of African-centred psychology, in particular therapeutic and psycho-educational forms of African psychology, is to break the cycle of anti-blackness, lack of self-acceptance and psychological violence.

What we should draw from the Clarks' work is that imperative which we need to take heed of more than any other: that each of us as African psychologists and students of psychology, today and tomorrow, if we are to leave the world a better place for the next generation, must say, today I start to love black, to learn black love; to value African children, because I value myself. Children can only really love and value themselves if they feel valued by the adults around them. They learn to love from seeing and learning how love is expressed by those adults. We accept ourselves, warts and all, if we are accepted by our fathers and mothers, warts and all. Of course this is hard. But this is what has to be done. Even if there are only a thousand African children who think that Africans are not as intelligent, talented and beautiful as Europeans, or that black people are not as creative as white people, shifting the preference of African children – and of black children from Europe, the US and other countries – away from predilections soaked in ideologies of white superiority and Euroamerican normativity remains a key challenge in the search for and effort to realise African-centred psychology.

18 | Search for Africa in psychology

My search for Africa in psychology was a search for a more welcoming home, a community for myself and later on for my students. What I found about Africa in psychology was ignorance, stereotypes, a dismissal of a whole continent of people in a sentence, or complete silence. When Africa was mentioned, it was an Africa neither I nor my students recognised. We could not relate. Partly because of this ignorance, absence, stereotyping and unrelatability, partly because it is really up to African scholars to write about the world from Africa as much as about Africa for the world, I gradually turned away from psychology towards studies on men and masculinities. From 2004 to 2007 my university formally agreed that I could divide my time between its Psychology Department and the Women's and Gender Studies Programme.

But for my own sanity I needed to draw the disparate elements of my work into a more coherent whole, with less jarring contradictions. Doing so was necessary to my health, and to the efficient use of my time and energy. I had to trace a clear connecting thread between psychology and masculinity. Searching for a home did not only mean finding a single university department or centre to contain my intellectual interests. It also meant trying to find what could be referred to as a disalienated identity, a certain way of *being in (a) place* where I would feel less like an interloper, less like an outsider; a way of being part of the world while being African. Specifically with respect to the question of Africa in psychology, it was a search for a way to be at home in a global psychology that is overwhelmingly dominated by US and Western European explanations, tools, concepts, therapeutic models and findings, and therefore can make someone who lives in an African country feel alienated. It is especially important to recognise that this was a search for a way of being black and yet ordinarily entitled, for want of a better concept, for I wanted the best and worst of all worlds. I like being black, but even in conditions where blackness becomes salient I am first and last always a man, not twice a man because of what men of my skin colour are enabled to see, and by no means half a man because of the history they have endured. A colourless person then, even though politically connected to a group, one prosaically entitled to be wherever he finds himself, to express his thoughts, sit with his feelings, act as he sees appropriate, love whom he wants, choose, ask questions, answer, fail or triumph, all of this being his right and attributable to him as a man and not to the group to which he belongs. I sought a way of conceiving, speaking or writing Africa, and the self that I am, as a natural part of the world.

My search for an unspectacularised, everyday kind of Africa in psychology compelled me to travel the world, instead of only reading about it. I regard myself as a reluctant traveller, to put it mildly. But I have a feeling that accepting invitations or availing myself of opportunities to attend academic meetings around the world is something one is expected to do to be a certain kind of thinker. I could be wrong. But I will say that travel, however unenthusiastic I am about it, has brought with it a certain fleshly kind of seeing the world in which I exist, a seeing which I now teach, a different kind of carnality in looking which enriches how I read, listen, write and love. It is a way of looking that one might oppose to an abstract way of seeing with the mind's eye from the library window, but such opposition is unnecessary because the body and its senses, feelings, spirit and thoughts are often great companions.

Consider as an example, then, this random selection of my travels over a decade, all of which are connected by the one question that constantly haunts me: how might we think Africa in this? For a number of years, around the mid-2000s, I participated as faculty in the Sexuality Leadership Development Fellowship organised by the African Regional Sexuality Resource Centre in Lagos, Nigeria. In June 2005 I gave a series of talks at the Council for the Development of Social Science Research in Africa (CODESRIA) Gender Institute in Dakar, Senegal. In September 2008 I agreed to give a series of Invited Lectures for a CODESRIA Sub-Regional Methodology Workshop on the Social Sciences in Africa, which was held in Gaborone, Botswana. In February 2009 I travelled to New Delhi, India, for the Hind Swaraj Centenary International Seminar. I participated in the Fifth European Conference on African Studies (ECAS) that took place at the Instituto Universitário de Lisboa (ISCTE-IUL) in Lisbon, Portugal, in June 2013. In October of that year I organised three panels at the International Conference on African Studies that took place at the University of Ghana in Accra, with the theme 'Revisiting the First International Congress of Africanists in a Globalised World'. A month later, I spoke about feminism for African boys at the 'Totta ja Tarua/Truths and Tales' Gender and Cultural Studies Conference, Rovaniemi, University of Lapland, Finland. In November 2014 I was a member of an invited panel at the Second Men Engage Global Symposium held at the India Habitat Centre, New Delhi. In February 2015 I was invited to Lake Naivasha in Kenya for the Conference on the State of the Art of Sexuality Research in Africa, where I presented a paper entitled 'The sex (talk) we want and the sex (talk) we might get'. A few months later, in July, I was at the Sorbonne in Paris, France, where I had travelled to participate in the Sixth ECAS and where I spoke on the topic of queering African traditions and liberating masculinities. In November 2015 I was at Princeton University in New Jersey, US, for the African Humanities Colloquium.

These are only some of the scores of symposia, workshops, conferences and meetings I attended outside of my country in the ten years between 2005 and 2015 whose expressed concern was not always Africa, but which made me think about how to think globally while being located in Africa. Bear in mind that this was a search that was not always articulated as such. And it has not been a search in a straight line, from A to B. In trying to find myself, there have been twists and turns. There is pushback, there are misses and many disappointments. And, like many other academics, I had other demands to satisfy such as teaching, marking papers, university meetings, public engagements, and more personal matters that needed my attention – any of which can end up being a detour that leads a person towards a different destination than the initial one towards which he set out.

I date the realisation that I had been searching for the right to say, without any sense of superiority or doubt, 'I see, precisely because I am from this part of the world,' to 2002, when I was preparing to give a public lecture at the Nordic Africa Institute, Uppsala, Sweden. There is no such right. But I am here again referring to a coming to consciousness of generative entitlement to the world; a positive sense of awareness of one's voice; a confidence in what one knows; and of course looking and looking back while being looked at. We should, however, always be wary of narratives of origins about the self or others, not only because narratives about the self never stay in one place, so that the self itself is not fixed, but also because memory is more fickle and malleable than we tend to allow. Let us therefore say, at the risk of oversimplifying matters, that this was one of the moments when I began to get a fuller, critical sense of how Africa is discoursed on, thought, taught, consumed, investigated. But, as I have said, the truth behind this is the disorientation I experienced about my place in the world, a disorientation that affects the voice, thinking, emotion, knowledge and experience itself; hence my search for a way out of this alienation had begun much earlier, during my first days as a university student.

Why do I participate in these conferences in Europe and the US (and not just stay in Africa), and what reason do I have to tell you of my travels? The reason is simple, yet significant: I was trained in psychology in South Africa. South African psychology has tended not to 'do' Africa, or to do it in a curious way; and South African psychology has had a historically strange relationship to the African continent, in contrast to its relationship with the US and Western Europe. A part of this strange historical relationship with Africa comes from the relationship that the country of South Africa has had with the African continent under colonialism and apartheid (and even after apartheid). South Africa considered itself as a place apart from Africa. Black Africa, as it was called, was regarded as essentially different from white South Africa. South African psychologists introjected and nourished this apartness, and essentialised the supposed difference of South Africa from the world of their counterparts from other African countries. Consequently, South African psychology came to be seen as not African psychology.

Another part of this strangeness is a result of the disorientation that occurs with regard to the meaning of the term 'African psychology' whenever it is mentioned, a point to which I have already referred. The term raises the question of what preposition is being elided between the two words 'psychology' and 'Africa'. Is the writer referring to all of psychology in or regarding Africa, or only psychology by African authors in Africa, or psychology on African subjects regardless of authorship, or psychology for

Africans? An additional consequence of the confusion is that while America and Europe are familiar to students, Africa is rarely ever mentioned, let alone taught, in psychology classes. To explicitly learn about Africa, a student or academic would need to venture into those fields traditionally seen as part of African studies, such as African history, African philosophy, African politics and African literature. (Here, in passing, I contend – again – that African psychology must be connected to these other fields in African studies.) My own adventures in trying to understand the situatedness of my work are therefore not unique, even though my interest in African studies (under whose umbrella I would in time get to develop what I have called psychological African studies) as a South African psychologist turned out be rather uncommon.

My search included turning my back on the discipline of psychology. Over time I found myself drawn to, and developed a specialisation in, the field of critical studies of men and masculinities. Critical studies of men and masculinities have tended to regard the problems of men and masculinities as better understood in terms of social rather than psychological conditions. There is, in fact, an area of men and masculinities studies in psychology, concentrated mainly in the US. Critical studies of men and masculinities, which tend to draw from sociological frameworks, the humanities, feminist theories, poststructuralism and other disciplines and sources beyond psychology, and which are more geographically dispersed and attract researchers from many countries, are also dominated by researchers in the rich West. While critical masculinities studies appear to be more welcoming to thinking about Africa when compared to psychology, the more established I have become in this field, the more I am struck by the absurdities of the ways in which Africa is taught or not taught, and Africans are studied or not studied, in both masculinities studies and psychology. I have become part of the absurdity, too often reproducing Africans as non-Europeans or non-Americans – as Others, strange or exotic – and Africa as only good for data collection or application.

Given that there is little presence – or an unfathomable presence – of Africa in psychology, while we have a thriving psychology and to a lesser extent field of masculinity studies in Africa, these travels I undertake are part of an ongoing search for more than simply a disalienated home for the psychological in studies of Africa. Three other motives have urged my pursuit. First, as I have said, I am interested in how Africa is taught, studied, hailed, constructed and consumed by Africans, Americans, Europeans and others across the globe. Second, I have been looking for points of productive convergence between psychology and other disciplines as taken up in and about Africa. Third, having remarked that scholars who work from a psychological perspective are scarce at conferences on African studies, I have felt that some of the topics under discussion at African studies conferences could benefit from African-centred psychological and psychoanalytic analyses.

In light of this, it is my intention to underscore the argument that there remains a need for African-centred psychology, even when we might feel happy with Western-centred psychology in Africa. The goal I have in mind is to contribute towards the development of a world-centred psychology conscious of its location in Africa – although maybe it is enough to merely cause a disruption, by drawing attention to the apparent widespread confusion about what is African about African psychology. Also, since my scholarship focuses mainly on men and masculinities, I intend – not here, but in the future – to contribute some thoughts on what one needs to do to become an African psychologist of boys, men and masculinities in a world where there is a psychology of African men yet there is no African-centred psychology of men.

It is my belief that in the continuing subjective and collective struggles for a centred African psychology, in the face of the persistent legacy of knowledge, being and power informed by coloniality, it is vital to encourage each other as psychologists to recount our own searches for, and hopefully attainment of, less self-othering voices.

It is also my belief that an existentially rewarding interest in both psychology and Africa cannot be at home in Africa without troubling itself with globally hegemonic traditions into which we, in Africa, are hailed as psychology students, teachers and researchers. That is to say, we cannot be completely at ease in our studies, as university teachers or as researchers in psychology, while facing up to the way Africa has been almost non-existent, nebulous, or unreal in the discipline of psychology. Neither can an interest in psychology and Africa be at ease in Euroamerican-centred psychology. A choice is forced upon our consciousness, or we have to live with the alienation.

The project to develop an African-centred psychology for the world, yet one conscious of its situatedness, is a project to which every awake psychologist in Africa interested in authentic living, relationships, research and teaching can contribute, and from which all can richly benefit.

Since the time of the travels described above, I have gone on to elaborate on some of these ideas in other lectures, symposia, seminars, colloquia and forums. I seem to be in the middle of re-membering and re-turning. I am remembering what excited me and led me into studying psychology in the first place. I am returning fully to psychology, to face up to why I became disenchanted with the discipline while I was right in the middle of work towards my master's degree. The unhappiness is not completely gone. But this project contains the sentiment that has brought me back to psychology, and has reinvigorated my faith in a psychology concerned with the well-being of all people, not just the mental health of those who can pay for their treatment, or who live in the middle-class suburbs of America or their imitations elsewhere.

Surely there remains a huge unrealised potential for psychology in Africa, for a psychology that enunciates from and about Africa. Although there may be others who feel happy with psychology as received from the West – and these happy psychologists include African psychologists and students, and they have every right to enjoy whatever kind of psychology they like – I believe I shall forever remain alienated until I work with others of like mind to build a world-centred, Africa-produced psychology.

Even more importantly, it seems that African psychologists like myself will remain irrelevant to the lives of most African people until we show our worth by helping primarily people in African countries, but also other people wherever they live in the world, to live authentic lives, characterised by healthy and meaningful relationships, with imagination unshackled, supported by dignified and rewarding work.

I wish someone had shown me the way back when I was in that master's class, because I wouldn't have wasted so much time on fancy but really not very useful academic fads.

19 | Dethingifying

Euroamerican psychology (in Africa) has been influenced by colonial power in Africa. That means, unconsciously or consciously, that those psychologists in Africa who are uncritical of Euroamerican-centred ideas are passively supportive of a history of ideas infected with colonialism.

In 1949, René Maunier (1887–1951), a member of the French Academy of Colonial Sciences and professor at the University of Paris, who is said to have been a sociologist of North Africa, wrote this:

> Colonisation is a contact of peoples. Apart from cases where wholly uninhabited territory has been occupied, the colonisers have come up against the earlier occupants, and have necessarily entered into relations with them: colonisation involves intercommunication. (Maunier 1949: 5–6)

Who believes this? Colonisation was no mere communication. Nor was it miscommunication. Colonisation was about the conquest of land and people. It was like an infection. It was about power, sometimes exercised in cruel and dehumanising ways. It was about control of populations and the colony.

There is more. Colonisation goes beyond the control of the colonised land and the bodies of the colonised. The coloniser always aims to extract anything of value from the colony for the benefit of those who wield power in the metropole or those who live in the white areas of the colony. Colonialism always reconfigures the economy and politics of the colony. At the same time, it rearranges pre-existing social and cultural structures in the colonised territory to support its economic aims. But here is what does not always receive full treatment – except by some radical thinkers in Africa and elsewhere: colonisation sets out to restructure the very behaviour, desires, interrelations and identities of the subject group and their colonisers, and succeeds in doing so. That is to say, it reconfigures the psychology of the individuals and the groups in the colony.

Can we see colonisation as intercommunication? No. As the anti-colonial Martiniquan poet and politician Aimé Césaire (1913–2008) said in his *Discourse on Colonialism*, first published in French in 1955, 'colonization = "thing-ification"'. Here, in a little more detail, is what he says to lead up to this structuring equation:

> I see clearly what colonization has destroyed: the wonderful Indian civilizations – and neither Deterding [an executive of the Royal Dutch Petroleum Company] nor Royal Dutch nor Standard Oil will ever console me for the Aztecs and the Incas.
>
> I see clearly the civilizations, condemned to perish at a future date, into which it has introduced a principle of ruin: the South Sea Islands, Nigeria, Nyasaland. I see less clearly the contributions it has made.
>
> Security? Culture? The rule of law? In the meantime, I look around and wherever there are colonizers and colonized face to face, I see force, brutality, cruelty, sadism, conflict, and, in a parody of education, the hasty manufacture of a few thousand subordinate functionaries, 'boys,' artisans, office clerks, and interpreters necessary for the smooth operation of business.
>
> I spoke of contact.
>
> Between colonizer and colonized there is room only for forced labor, intimidation, pressure, the police,

taxation, theft, rape, compulsory crops, contempt, mistrust, arrogance, self-complacency, swinishness, brainless elites, degraded masses.

No human contact, but relations of domination and submission which turn the colonizing man into a classroom monitor, an army sergeant, a prison guard, a slave driver, and the indigenous man into an instrument of production.

My turn to state an equation: colonization = 'thingification'. (Césaire 1972: 6)

If colonisation 'thingifies', an element of African-centred psychology must be to act as a *dethingifying* force. African-centred psychology has to be a project to decolonise the mind, affect and body, to enable Africans to be perfectly entitled to their experiences and to be in the world as it appears in their consciousness.

20 | Three problems

To seek to entrench African-centred psychology is a quest to better locate Africa and Africans in knowledge. To try to locate Africans better means to situate them in less stereotypical ways, to produce ideas that are disalienating for a meaningful life in Africa. 'Disalienating ideas' refers to those ideas whose underlying, if not always articulated, object is to situate Africa as a place of knowledge-making for the world and to locate Africans as theory makers, not only data creators. This object encompasses investigation of the very question of what knowledge itself is, as well as of its dissemination – the building of publics for the knowledge we create as researchers, teachers, students, professionals, policymakers, or activists. The primary question that we must deal with in African-centred knowledge is therefore always about the location of knowledge and being, as well as of power, after the facts of colonialism, slavery and apartheid.

The future of African-centred psychology does not lie in repeating the demand for it to exist alongside Euroamerican-centred psychology. It lies in doing many more research studies centring Africa. Large as well as in-depth studies. Theoretical work that situates itself within cultures and institutions in Africa while generating explanations that have global meaning. It lies in unapologetically situating the fact of being in Africa in our lecture rooms, in university policies, in professional networks and associations. In understanding the self as deeply 'affected' by being of Africa and situated in a place in Africa. All this we have to do if we are to extricate ourselves from the enduring effects of colonial, slavocratic and apartheid systems of power, feeling, thought and being.

There are, however, three problems that confront psychologists and students in trying to see the world, their work and themselves from an African centre.

The first problem we face as psychologists or students in trying to think, teach, heal, learn, feel, or work while keeping Africa at the centre of the world is precisely how colonialism comes to reshape knowledge about what it means to be human. As part of the colonial and apartheid intellectual arsenal, psychology was weaponised, along with other sciences, towards the making of a certain understanding of Africans, who came to be thought of as black, as a different species of humans. No, as a lower form of life: that is why we have to say, black lives matter. The principal attachment to the use of race as a so-called variable is a residue of the belief that whites and blacks are essentially different groups of human beings; it is not a recognition that racial difference is created by structural conditions – colonisation, slavery, racism and apartheid being principal among them – that favour one group over another.

Psychology, like other disciplines as they arrive in Africa, is organised in such a way that it dismisses what Africans know. Psychology as received is designed to question how Africans look at themselves, and to not question those who would be their masters. Psychology, as it leaves Europe and the US and comes to Africa, is structured in such a way as to make Africans forget what they think or feel, coercing, seducing or rewarding them for valuing European and American interpretations of their dreams (and the rest of their life conditions, of course) over their own interpretations.

The second problem we confront in trying to think psychologically from a place in Africa derives from a powerful assumption – an assumption that is tied to the power of location: that the world looks the same wherever you stand in it.

This assumption is often confused with the idea of universality, when the fact is that American and European – not universal – ideas about human psychology dominate us. That is what makes them dominate how we think of psychology in Africa. The assumption that the world looks the same wherever you stand in it, which is conflated with the notion of universal knowledge, is what informs the argument that, for instance, child development or love must mean the same whether you are in London or Lilongwe.

We know that pluriversality is what Walter Mignolo (2005, 2010) sees as the answer to the imperial universalisation of the concept of universality. Pluriversality conveys the idea that the world can have many coexisting world views. I see the answer in learning to see the world from Africa, with Africa as the centre from which we project, while remaining open to the fact that the world probably looks different to others, depending on their positions in the universe.

The third problem is that of the disembodied author of knowledge. The author of psychological knowledge – the one who has authority – was most often based in the metropole, and is now in the urban centres of the global north. Looking first towards the global north for answers to problems found in the global south is what generates what the Beninois philosopher Paulin Hountondji (1987) has called 'scholarly extraversion' – an attitude to knowledge that leads many African researchers to be tempted to address themselves to non-African publics, and leads also to their subordination to global northern markets of knowledge.

21 | Fog and friction

Let us return to the question, what does it mean to say *African* in African psychology ought to be unspoken? What, precisely, is African psychology?

To better appreciate the answers to these questions, let us begin with the second question first.

Confusion abounds within and around the meaning of African psychology. One answer to the question is: African psychology is not American psychology. That much is clear. Another answer: African psychology is not European psychology. That is obvious too.

Beyond that – we have fog and friction.

I know why European and US psychologists – as well as Euroamerican-centred psychologists in Africa and elsewhere outside of Europe and the US – who subscribe to psychology as seen from Euroamerican psychological perspectives might be confused. Because of their own confusion they are usually confusing when they try to say something about African psychology. To believe that African psychology is a special type of psychology is to be confused.

I know why much of what is written by African and African American psychologists who champion African psychology also does not make the concept easy to comprehend. Euroamerican psychology has been very effective in creating a great deal of the confusion among African students, therapists and teachers and the general public, let alone among white European and US students, teachers and therapists. One of the major confusions is that Euroamerican psychology is psychology, and anything else is (blank) psychology – where (blank) stands for any 'indigenous', othered and supposedly non-standard psychology which is not real psychology. Euroamerican psychology, apparently, is indigenous to nowhere. It is a body of knowledge with neither origin nor home.

Regarding the first question, African in African psychology is what exists, at the best of times, when African psychology is not on the defensive, a term in brackets: (African) psychology. In other words, when African psychology is psychology. Paradoxically, the best African psychology is therefore knowledge and practice that begin from consciousness-raising about ways of seeing people's lives – from the birth of a baby to the moment of death – through Africa's window; knowledge and practice that, over time, become unconscious. The best African psychological perspective is one that has settled at the unselfconscious level and does not name itself. African psychology is about fully appreciating your own world on this very large continent of more than a billion people of different countries, languages, ethnicities, hues, religions and classes, as well as the place of Africa in the world. African psychology is at its best when, having become habitual, it takes its own voice for granted.

African psychology is not essentially unlike psychology from Asia, Australia, Europe, Latin America, North America, or anywhere else in the world: we all study humans. To name psychology as African springs from a desire to extend ourselves, as African psychologists and students, beyond the established borders of traditional psychology. To put psychology after African is also to want to instigate investigation of topics that are of interest to Africans but are usually not studied by Euroamerican psychologists. It may be that such topics are of interest to people in Europe and the US, too; but, because of what psychologists in those parts of the world think of as psychology, they are probably topics occluded from the view of many in those countries.

22 | African enough?

The Forum for African Psychology (FAP) was founded in 2009 as a division of the Psychological Society of South Africa. The establishment of the FAP followed long-standing debates on the object of African psychology, its definition, its status, its aims and its approaches. The FAP's founding has reignited these debates. But there is still often more heat than light produced about what African psychology is. There is confusion as to why we might or might not need to develop students and young researchers who are conscientised to be unselfconscious about their African psychological perspective.

Is it not ludicrous, a confused alien could well ask, do we need an African psychology forum in South Africa?

An answer the alien might receive is, we need such a forum because South Africa is not African enough.

Or, because the Psychological Society of South Africa is not African enough.

The question becomes, what is it to be African enough in a place like South Africa, in contrast to places like Somalia and Senegal?

23 | Antipathy, apathy

There is old ill will towards anything African, no doubt – hostility which seeps into African-centred psychology.

Lack of enthusiasm about the need for African-centred psychology is also not unknown. Nor are disapprobation and denial of the need for such a thing, even while its nature is misconstrued.

The antipathy and apathy towards African psychology coming from psychology students, teachers and professionals stems from old and contemporary feelings and arguments against the idea of Africa and the blackness – signalling darkness, dirt, ugliness, evil – that is said to inhere in Africans. And yet I am constantly startled by the intelligence, the triumph over adversity, the resilience, the beauty and innovation, the music, storytelling and laughter, the deep love and knowledge of the land, the incredible readiness to forgive, as well as the density of life, that exist on a continent some have seen as nothing but an area of darkness.

24 | Superhuman subhuman

The black, you might know, was the first superhuman.

The black was the slave – no thought, no emotions, no volition. The black was property.

A workhorse, the slave appears human but is not.

The black has a different psychology.

The black, a fear-inducing thing, needs to be kept under watch.

Why is the black afraid? The black is not supposed to be afraid. The black makes others afraid.

The black, no feelings.

The black cannot be raped.

The black, rapist.

The black, lazy.

The black is a sex machine.

The black machine.

Superman is not human. Superhuman is subhuman. Superhuman, subhuman, monstrosities.

Against this black-cloth, how to create a positive psychology of blacks?

25 | Sources of negativity

Some of the negative opinions and sentiments about African-centred psychology are expressed by individuals. Some of the negativity is observable in institutional arrangements, such as what is taught in psychology departments, and who is recruited into professional clinical, counselling, organisational and educational psychology programmes. Ironically, some of the negativity comes from unexpected quarters, like black psychologists.

26 | Not all (blacks) think alike

Why, though, I have to remind myself once again, would we expect all black psychologists to understand and love black-centred and African-centred psychology – unless we are once again tripped up by the racist belief that all blacks think alike, feel alike, even if they do not look like?

Where we are seduced into expecting that all black psychologists will be keen on psychology that centres blacks, the corollary is that all white psychologists represent white supremacist Euroamerican-centred psychology. This is not borne out by my experience. There are many white allies who support pluriversal (which is not the same as universal), world-centred ways of knowing and knowledges, and oppose an oppressive knowledge that privileges supremacist whiteness.

The implication? It takes a certain political and ethical consciousness, not race, to grasp the global flows of knowledge, the relations between power and knowledge.

27 | Causes of confusion

What causes all the confusion regarding African-centredness in psychology?

I have already mentioned the usual suspects: economic domination, colonial attitudes, racism, marginalisation.

The generous part of my being thinks the confusion around African psychology and African-centred psychology may be due to plain old lack of education and obfuscation.

And then, at different moments, in various ways, among individuals within the groups that have been at the receiving end of Euroamerican psychology, I encounter self-delusion, feelings of personal power in people's own little dominion, or lack of imagination perhaps. Not every little bit of the confusion and lack of fervour for African-centred psychology flows out of misunderstanding, colonial sentiments and contemporary anti-black racism.

Yet there is little doubt in my mind that some of the apparent confusion is really about prejudice and hypocrisy. Both arise from coloniality and the discrimination that springs from a deeply embedded racism, in institutions and persons. It would be a grave error to believe that colonial and racist structures and attitudes are things of the past. I am concerned that, above all, for a certain category of students and teachers and professionals, the cause of the confusion begins with how we imagine African psychology as a whole – that is to say, what we imagine when the words 'African psychology' are uttered, what is African and what is psychology in African psychology, what are its boundaries and horizons, and what are its internal and necessary differences.

Perhaps the most intractable issue is that of alienation. Alienation compounds the confusion surrounding African psychology.

There are several scholars who have written on the idea of alienation, such as Karl Marx, Georg Simmel, Erich Fromm and Frantz Fanon. But let us begin with some basic definitions. A standard dictionary definition of alienation is 'the act of estranging or state of estrangement in feeling or affection; loss of mental faculties; the act of transferring ownership of anything; diversion of something to a different purpose' (Brown 1993: 51).

Alienation exercised Fanon a great deal. In *Toward the African Revolution*, he states:

> Having witnessed the liquidation of its systems of reference, the collapse of its cultural patterns, the native can only recognize with the occupant that 'God is not on his side'. The oppressor, through the inclusive and frightening character of his authority, manages to impose on the native *new ways of seeing*, and in particular *a pejorative judgment with respect to his original forms of existing*. This event, which is commonly designated as alienation, is naturally very important. It is found in the official texts under the name of assimilation. (Fanon 1967: 38; emphasis mine)

Alienation distorts our vision. It infects our existence. It induces us to disapprove of ourselves, to regard our ways of living, now seen as inferior when compared to those of the oppressor, in deprecatory terms.

Someone else who had something to say about alienation was Bantu Stephen Biko. In the trial of members of the South African Students' Congress and Black People's Convention (organisations designated illegal by the apartheid government) in May 1976, Biko, under cross-examination, made this connection between alienation and what the philosophy of Black Consciousness was meant to achieve with respect to black manhood:

> I think basically Black Consciousness refers itself to the black man and to his situation, and I think the black man is subjected to two forces in this country. He is first of all oppressed by an external world through institutionalised machinery, through laws that restrict him from doing certain things, through heavy work conditions, through poor pay, through very difficult living conditions, through poor education, these are all external to him, and secondly, and this we regard as the most important, the black man in himself has developed a certain state of *alienation*, he rejects himself, precisely because he attaches the meaning white to all that is good, in other words he associates good and he equates good with white. This arises out of his living and it arises out of his development from childhood. (Biko 1987: 100; emphasis mine)

I am also in agreement with what the British critical psychologist Ian Parker (2007: 5) has written about alienation:

> Alienation is not merely the separation of ourselves from others but a kind of separation from ourselves in which we experience ourselves as inhabited and driven by forces that are mysterious to us. These mysterious

forces include economic forces that structure our lives
as beings who must sell our labour to others.

African psychology as a whole is in the upside-down state it is
because the bulk of psychology in Africa is alienating; it does not
address the experiential life of those who may be most in need of
what psychology could offer them, but does not.

Not only many students but teachers and therapists as
well are estranged from their true concerns by Euroamerican
psychology. There are very few who speak in their original
voice. Especially when they arrive at university, psychology
students are taught to rely excessively on authorities who are
usually somewhere in the US and Europe. They are induced
to forget their own inborn voice and creativity, and why they
wanted to do psychology in the first place. This happens because
many of their teachers, too, have transferred ownership of how
to understand the mental and emotional lives of people around
them to these authorities. The teachers were never taught to
teach African psychology. Many teachers, and also therapists,
are therefore not authors of their own explanations. They mimic
how the Euroamerican authorities explain the contents of the
mind and emotions and relationships. They teach the same
ability for mimicry to their students, rather than coming up with
contextually sound therapeutic explanations. It is sad. But that is
precisely what coloniality has managed to achieve.

You can see why the challenge facing us is nothing less
than to regain our mental faculties so as to be able to account
for the psyche – certainly our own psyche – from an African-
centred psychological perspective. To make sense of an issue –
for instance, a personality-related problem, or a problem of
communication, depression, attachment, shame, lack of trust, or
learning – from an African-centred psychological perspective

means making sense of it from the perspective of the daily life we live with others. Consider these questions as examples of the lives I may be talking about, and guess if these are common questions in psychology textbooks produced in Western Europe and the US: (a) How might we understand how a child becomes the top student in the country, having grown up in a one-roomed shack with her mother, grandmother, siblings, nephews and cousins? (b) If someone is raped, but lives quite a distance from a health facility, his family lives in a neighbourhood rife with violence where many rapes have occurred, and the family is dependent on a social grant, what is the role of the therapist in this situation, and how is the young man to be helped?

29 | The centre

The notion of centre, of centredness, or what Molefi Kete Asante (1991) refers to as centricity, is key to my efforts to contribute towards African-centred psychology. In his article 'The Afrocentric idea in education' published in *The Journal of Negro Education*, Asante writes: 'centricity refers to a perspective that involves locating students within the context of their own cultural references so that they can relate socially and psychologically to other cultural perspectives' (1991: 171). I have come to see how I have walked some of the same paths walked by other black scholars in African countries and in America, like Asante; I feel cheated, I am afraid, for not having known the notions of centricity and Afrocentricity when I was struggling with my voice, perspective and sense of alienation while teaching psychology, between October 1996 and April 2004.

In the same article Asante observes 'that the most productive method of teaching any student is to place his or her group within the center of the context' (1991: 171). In my view this is a self-evident truth, and hence something with which I totally agree – the utter significance of locating a student and his or her values and material structures of living at the centre of the context of learning. Learning is decidedly easier if students can relate the new content to something in their lives. It is hard to see something in your mind if you cannot *see* it, and even more so if you have no view of yourself. As Asante says in his book *An Afrocentric Manifesto*, Afrocentricity 'is a theory of agency, the idea that African people must be viewed and view themselves as agents rather than spectators to historical revolution and change' (2007: 17).

What I bring to psychology with the idea of being centred is that it is not applicable only to teaching and learning. A centred psychology, a centring of Africa in psychology, applies to research too. The first thing you start to appreciate when you wish to conduct a study from an African-centred psychological perspective is that the least alienating of light is cast on your topic and your participants if you place what philosophers refer to as lived experiences of the participants – their personal accounting of their own experiences – at the centre of your study. You do not place the stereotypes, or the imagined lives, or previous findings from a study conducted on college students in the US, or what is called theory, before your subjects (although previous research and explanations of the phenomena of interest do have to enter the picture at some point).

The idea of centredness applies to psychotherapy too, of course. Consider that if you talk to many students in educational, counselling and clinical psychology – and I do – they will tell you that, even though the course is intensive and great, they have found very little about Africa – that is to say, about their own experiences as African students – in the course. This is not to say that the faculty is bad, out to deliberately alienate the students. Many of the teachers have not had the kind of education where Africa is at the centre. They have not learned the languages spoken by the majority of students. They use teaching material from the US and Western Europe. As a result, the students have to find out for themselves how to do therapy with what some texts call 'non-traditional' clients. 'Traditional clients' in this case refers to middle-class persons seeking therapy, usually speaking English and able to pay for their treatment. 'Non-traditional client' is therefore a misnomer, when the majority of people cannot pay and cannot speak English. Language is perhaps the most vital clue as to why the majority of Africa is not at the centre of psychotherapy as it is taught, learned and practised on the continent. If psychotherapy is a talking cure, how do you talk to a people when you cannot speak their tongue?

Centring implies that the first thing you start to appreciate when you wish to do psychotherapy from a cultural, African-centred psychological perspective is that you must learn the language of the person you are seeking to help. Meaning resides in words. Without the right words we are really lying to each other. Without knowing what the other person could have said if given a chance to speak in his or her language, you are being dishonest about what relief you can bring. You are deluding yourself. You are not being honest.

The least alienating of light is cast on the presenting problem if the clinical or educational psychologist places the meaning-making of the patient or difficulties of the school-child at the centre. And along with the centring of the meaning the person makes of his or her life, you as the psychologist must place yourself, your own values, beliefs and assumptions about life, relationships and identity, at the centre. This is what centring involves. Anything less than readiness to be open, to be honest, about how you understand people is quite farcical. But this waste of time and pretence happens all the time in hospital wards, clinics and therapy rooms.

So, centring means building psychology departments, research groups, or professional networks in which we try as much as possible to situate at their centre the languages and experiences and relationships and subjectivities of the people with whom we are working.

30 | Terminology

We have touched on some terms already. Here are other key terms of which to take note, with brief descriptions:

Western/Euroamerican psychology: Western or Euroamerican psychology is all psychology concerning Europe and the US. Euroamerican-oriented psychology is found not only in the US and European countries but all over the world, including Africa. It dominates Africa and the rest of the world. Euroamerican psychology in Africa is also what at times I refer to as psychology-*in*-Africa (which is to be understood as different from psychology *for* Africa) in my framework of four orientations in African psychology presented in section 82. Euroamerican psychology puts the experiences of mainly white, Western European and US, middle- to upper-class, usually heterosexual men and women, but also lesbian, gay, bisexual, transgender, queer and intersexed (LGBTQI) Westerners, at the centre of its world. Even when it is exported to Africa, Western-centred psychology ultimately serves the economic, political and cultural ends of Europe and the US. In the most general terms, mainstream Euroamerican psychology tends to assume (and, based on this assumption, to pose questions, design studies, make interpretations, offer psychotherapies and prescribe psycho-pharmacological medication that support the assumption) that life experiences have to be better and more satisfying in the capitals of Western Europe and America for a certain economic class of people. Conversely, people in their right mind – meaning psychologically healthy – cannot really have a full, meaningful and satisfying life in Africa or other parts of the world, certainly not if they are money-poor (in contrast to spiritually poor, for example) and do not subscribe to assumptions underpinning mainstream Euroamerican psychology. 'Euroamerican psychological research has for long served as a rationalising bulwark,' the great Somali psychologist Hussein Abdilahi Bulhan (1980: 20) observed, 'stifling consciousness as well as conscience regarding the ruthless exploitation of the African.'

African psychology: There are some people, such as my colleagues at the University of KwaZulu-Natal (UKZN) – and it is worth mentioning here Nhlanhla Mkhize and Augustine Nwoye – who apparently hold the view that African psychology is a field in psychology (see Mkhize 2004; Nwoye 2015). More specifically, they seem to consider African psychology as a branch of psychology, similar to how psychologists usually think of developmental psychology, neuropsychology, or social psychology.

My inference as to how UKZN psychologists view African psychology is derived from the fact that this university offers a number of courses in African psychology. I can appreciate the need for different tactics to be used to make African psychology ordinary, which might involve putting African psychology on the curriculum and having a course named 'African Psychology 101'. I am aware that it is often a tremendous battle to succeed in having something called 'PSYC345 African Psychology' on the curriculum. Given the pervasive disorientation and alienation perceptible in university curricula, institutional traditions and cultures, and policies and structures in universities, I can imagine that it could be taken as an achievement to have a university agree to a course on 'Advanced Topics in African Psychology'. I believe this tactic is not, however, the best way to proceed in order to place Africa and Africans at the centre of psychology, especially that psychology taught in African universities and employed in hospitals and consulting rooms across Africa. Primarily, my objection is that any explicit reference to Africa and Africans in the names of the courses in psychology is a form of self-imposed othering. It is completely ridiculous, self-objectifying and self-marginalising to have a course called 'African Psychology' being offered at all in a psychology department in a university in Africa. Of course, the fact of colonialism is implicated in these absurdities, and in what can be called 'psychology of the third person'. Of course, coloniality persists, still making some of us cling to privileged Western perspectives on what we do and what we feel and what we think. The ideology of Western supremacy is what generates such forms of self-othering, certainly. And yes, of course, the cultural and economic displacement of Africa in the global knowledge economy, and of poor and underclass Africans, continues to a large degree.

However, the fact is that a number of those who identify with Africa and as Africans now occupy powerful positions in the professoriate in universities in Africa – and elsewhere around the world. We are department heads, we are heads of schools, we are deans, we are vice-chancellors. Depending on our imagination and labour, things can be changed fundamentally or cosmetically. We are in a position to change the university. So why other ourselves? If it is the case that a number of black and white Africa-identified psychologists are in positions where we are able to effect basal change that can reflect the deepest inner-directed yearnings of our lives, instead of re-imposing Western-imposed views of Africa on our students – change that leads to Africa and the lived experiences of most Africans being reflected in what students learn and what we teach – the question is, why reproduce the colonial othering of Africans?

There is something essential here with which we have to come to terms: the meaning of being at the centre, the persistence of our own self-abjection. Appreciating being at the centre means that Africa-identified psychologists, all of whom are in positions of heft or influence, have to come to terms with the reality of their sway. That power may be limited or weighty; it may be power over a client, in front of a class, or at the head of a department or research centre. Regardless, by virtue of their profession, qualification or position, they have influence. Coming to terms with their clout means realising that they are in a position to transform the world of psychology – and of their departments, if they are employed in universities; to reform these institutions in some little way; or to basically leave things as they are, except for their presence there as individuals. It means recognising the need to pluralise the centres of psychology, to universalise psychology from Africa. Being in Africa – or teaching in America or Europe – Africa-identified psychologists have to consciously seek, to take a phrase from Ngũgĩ wa Thiong'o (1993), to move the centre of global psychology – or they will always remain interlopers, or reproduce the notion of Africa as a marginal presence.

An implication – and there are several – of this commitment to moving the centre is that Africa-identified psychologists can construct courses and design curricula that are wholly embedded in, and fundamentally shaped by, the experiential lives, economies, politics, institutions and many cultures of this continent. Another implication is that it becomes necessary to redesign and reconfigure what is taught at universities, work that has to include utterly rethinking the departmentalisation of knowledge.

The most significant criticism that can be made of the tactics employed by UKZN psychologists is that they are effectively not admitting that African psychology refers to all psychology concerning Africa. African psychology can be pursued and produced by Africans as well as non-Africans, in Africa and beyond. What is needed is not 'African Psychology 101' but (African-centred) 'Psychology 101', (African-centred) 'Psychology 345', or 'Advanced Topics in (African-centred) Psychology'.

What does this mean? It means that Africa and Africans are the tacit centre of all your courses, if not of how your whole department and university are structured – including its policies, the academic texts used to teach, its cultural climate, the values inculcated in the graduates, the knowledge produced, and the products created. It means that all courses offered in a department such as psychology (or statistics, microbiology, pathology, or astronomy), indeed the entire curriculum in a university, locates Africa at the centre – just as life in Africa is at the centre of the world from which we think, eat, see, learn about who we are, study, know love, feel unloved, work, marry, fight, divorce, get depressed, bear children, play, abandon children, achieve success and die.

However, it is common cause that not all psychology, including that offered in African universities, places Africa at the centre. This is what UKZN, and those other institutions that would offer courses such as 'Advanced Topics in African Psychology' in a psychology department in an African university, are seeking to change by inserting African psychology courses into the curriculum.

Having become aware of the reach of apartheid and coloniality, we ought not to be aghast at the realisation that some African psychologists, in Africa, unconsciously or wilfully replicate oppressive notions about Africa derived from Europe and the US – although it is still a realisation that stuns. We should not be amazed, but we are still baffled, to find that some Africans can and do deliberately or blindly perpetuate negative stereotypes about Africans. Euroamerican psychology has conquered the world.

African-centred psychology: It bears repeating: African-centred psychology is psychology that centres Africa and Africans. The main difference between the broader concept of African psychology as all of psychology practised in Africa, whether by Africans or non-Africans, and African-centred psychology is precisely that at the core of African-centred psychology lie Africa and Africans. Whether Africans are the therapists or the clients, the teachers or the students, the researchers or the researched, African-centred psychology approaches Africa and Africans from their perspectives.

Black psychology: Black psychology is a field of thought developed by black Americans to focus on black people, with its origins dating to the 1960s. Black psychology is a part of black studies (Asante & Mazama 2005; Karenga 1988; Marable 2000; Rojas 2007). Black psychological studies still find their most trenchant and best expression among black American psychologists (Baldwin 1986; Cokley et al. 2013; Jackson 1982; Nobles 2013). Black psychology as a field is almost non-existent in Africa.

Black psychology overlaps with African psychology. Some African American psychologists like Wade Nobles (1991), Na'im Akbar (1984) and Joseph Baldwin (1986) have sought to show that black psychology is best considered as identical with African psychology. But do all black American psychologists identify with African psychology, as distinct from African American psychology? Should psychologists in Africa see black psychology as one and the same thing as African psychology?

Black-centred psychology: While black American psychologists were creating black psychology, somewhere in Africa a lonely voice (as Cyril Couve wrote in 1986) was trying to write a psychology of black experience: the pioneering Noel Chabani

Manganyi. Yet, black psychology never took off in Africa; this is a quirk in the development of psychology in African countries that still deserves scrutiny. I suspect that among the reasons for this is the reservation felt by African psychologists about why, if the predominantly white countries do not have an expressly white psychology (if white is quiet in white psychology), a largely black continent should need a black psychology. This despite the fact that it is common knowledge among critical, radical and anarchist thinkers that, in addition to its positive regard for the upper and middle classes, the globally hegemonic type of psychology has for the longest time been unabashedly white.

What I would like for us to do is to introduce blackness at the centre of global psychology, alongside African psychology. Centring blackness in psychology implies a black-centred psychology. A black-centred psychology looks white psychology (which can admit its whiteness only under duress – even if it then chooses to continue on its miserable way) in the face, takes full cognisance of the fact that whiteness has ruled our psychological world, and aims to challenge this state of affairs.

A black-centred psychology looks at the world through black eyes. It focuses on black joy and pain, achievements and losses, slavery, racism and overcoming. Black-centred psychology is a blood relative of African-centred psychology. And of course, African-centred psychology has a black soul. There are times like the ones in which we are living – the times of racism, of Donald Trump, of right-wing movements in Europe – or other times (of Nazism and apartheid) – when psychologists who appreciate the need for seeing with black eyes, for looking at the world with the benefit of black experience, will have to be the mothers of African-centred psychology. Sometimes African-centred psychologists, those who would centralise the fact of living in Africa and carrying an African passport, will have to father black centres of psychology. Black-centred psychology, then, situates black lives and black expertise at the centre of its enterprise.

31 | Defining by negation

Seven things that, in my framework, African psychology is not:

1. African psychology is not a discipline outside of psychology.
2. African psychology is not a sub-discipline of psychology.
3. African psychology is not a specific area of study, such as the study of traditional African healing practices.
4. African psychology is not only a psychology practised on Africans.
5. African psychology is not only a psychology practised by Africans.
6. African psychology is not only for Africans.
7. African psychology is not only from Africa; like Euroamerican psychology, it can be taught at European universities, can be dramatised in US television sitcoms, can be applied in therapy rooms in Australia.

32 | Self-sabotage

An African-centred psychologist can say, 'I study cognitive development from an African perspective,' of course. But the moment you utter those words, despite your conscious intention, you have already betrayed your unconscious wish and real desire. Your real desire is to persuade the audience of the rightness of your study. Your unconscious wish is for your view to be accepted. As such, you have undermined the potential influence of your study. And you will be rejected.

The argument that when a female researcher feels compelled to state (to give another example), 'My master's study looked at stress among first-generation middle-class women and men from an *African* feminist perspective,' she has already undermined the potential influence of her study, arises from the knowledge that the most likely question that follows her declaration is not, 'What did you find?' but rather, 'What is an *African* feminist perspective?' This is not necessarily an unwelcome question if you are developing an African feminist perspective. But it may be distressing when you wish to talk about stress, and that is the main question in which your audience is interested.

33 | A welcoming home

There is an undeniable desire for African-centred psychology in Africa, certainly in South Africa. This is the desire to return to and learn to appreciate the history of the work done by African scholars on the continent and in the diaspora. It's a desire stimulated by feelings and perceptions of alienated expertise. It arises from the question, what does it mean to be a highly qualified professional educational, clinical, child, social, counselling, developmental, cognitive, cultural, or any other kind of psychologist you can think of, to be invited to conferences around the world to share your expertise, when in your gut you feel that yours is a body out of place, an impostor, that you are an alien not entitled to be there?

An alienated expert is a mimic. Alienated expertise means the expert is not the originator of the knowledge he or she professes.

The implication of all this is that there is an imperative for you to build – in psychology, in your lecture rooms and departments, in your consulting rooms, in your books and articles and films, in your activism and psychological art, and in the spaces in which you work and interact – a more welcoming home. You are compelled, unless you want to remain enslaved by Euroamerican ideas, to liberate your mind and work and practices from the colonial and apartheid master's gaze. To build an authentic African psychology. To strengthen African-centred psychology coming out of African countries, by building on the history of African thought (as well as non-African thought which challenges the injustice ferried around the world as part of the global hegemony of Euroamerican-centrism).

34 | Defining by affirmation

Ten things you ought to know about African-centred psychology:

1. African-centred psychology is about seeing.
2. African-centred psychology is about language.
3. African-centred psychology is knowledge that begins with an inward-looking process, with speaking not about yourself but about the world as you have come to know it.
4. African-centred psychology is a reawakening, a road towards emancipation, a project that encompasses emotional, cognitive, cultural, political and economic attitudes and practices.
5. African-centred psychology is a call to rid yourself of the shackles of intellectual servitude to Euroamerican-centred knowledge.
6. African-centred psychology is the antithesis of oppressive knowledge about Africa and Africans.
7. African-centred psychology is about consciously and intelligently placing Africa at the centre of your psychological work.
8. African-centred psychology is attentive to history.
9. African-centred psychology is resistance.
10. African-centred psychology is a position in psychology, not something outside of it, even though it can exceed received psychology, even though it has to push beyond the boundaries of Euroamerican-dominated global psychology by studying topics of significance to people in Africa, producing therapeutic techniques that work for the greatest number of people in Africa, and *teaching psychology* about Africa.

35 | Scholarly extraverts and introverts

When thinking about African psychology nuance is warranted, and distinctions have to be made with respect to how individuals are oriented towards Africa and psychology. The major distinction to be drawn turns on the centre of gravity of your work as a psychologist in Africa. We need to differentiate between Euroamerican-centrists on the one hand and African-centrists on the other.

The two categories of African psychologists can also be called scholarly *extraverts* and scholarly *introverts* – terms adapted from the work of Paulin Hountondji (1987). These terms do not refer to personality. Scholarly extraverts look to the theories and models and problems arising in the global north to guide their ontological, epistemological, methodological and technical interests. Scholarly introverts look to the experiences and realities, streets and paths in their countries for their ontological, epistemological, methodological and technical interests.

36 | It's African, except when it's not

The idea of African psychology appears to be a straightforward matter, I have said, except when it is not. And the latter, not the former, is usually the state of affairs.

It may be easy to comprehend that all of psychology done in and for Africa, about Africans, by Africans as well as non-Africans (working on topics related to Africa and Africans) is of course African psychology. However, confusion is introduced when psychologists in Africa regard themselves as not African psychologists. It would seem logical that psychologists working in Europe are European psychologists. (Except, that is, those psychologists who hold Yemeni, Nigerian or Argentinian passports, or who identify with their birth countries outside of the European community even though they may have acquired citizenship of a European country, or who are stateless, or who live in other circumstances that could nullify the professional identity 'European psychologist'.)

Similarly, it would seem logical that psychologists working in Africa are African psychologists. Except that it is not. One explanation is that some psychology teachers, researchers and therapists simply do not identify with Africa. A lot of work is required to undo the miseducation that created such teachers, researchers and therapists. Others feel ambivalent about their own fortunes being tied to the fortune of Africa. Some hope exists that positive light can be cast on such ambivalence. Still others, especially students and younger psychologists, may be disoriented, fearful, or lack knowledge about Africa. Among the three explanations, this is the one in which the greatest hope for the future of African psychology is to be found.

37 | Points on a continuum

Making the distinction between scholarly extraversion and introversion in African psychology is a way to reflect on the term 'centring'. Scholarly extraversion and introversion are two end points of a continuum. The confusion and battles within African psychology revolve around the question of how psychologists might be able to locate themselves on this continuum.

To one side you find a psychologist who sees relatively little wrong with much of the psychology that she practises, or with many of the approaches to teaching and research that she employs, or with many of the therapeutic healing practices she uses on her clients. The thing is that, even though some of us may suspect that the way we live and where we work contribute, by omission if not commission, to socioeconomic injustice, or that the discipline of psychology is dominated by US and Western European patriarchal capitalist interests, we may feel that we are better off with the world of psychology as it is. Ironically, those who see nothing fundamentally off-colour with much of psychology as it is, include those of us who identify as social-justice-oriented psychologists. We may recognise and critique what is wrong with mainstream, non-critical, hegemonic psychology and its methods and explanations. But we do hold very dearly to, and our differentiation is marked by, our knowledge of our Brownmillers, Butlers and Cixouses, our Chomskys, De Beauvoirs and Derridas, our Du Boises, Foucaults and Lacans. That is to say, we privilege the major critical and radical European and US thinkers, be they male, female, or other genders/sexes, white, black, brown, or of other racially or ethnically defined groups. The centre of gravity of this offshore model of African psychology is Europe and the US. As an offshore, extraverted psychology, this African psychology primarily looks to places outside of the continent for legitimation and reward, using the locals mainly as a site of data extraction or application. This African psychology might be taught and written in some African universities, but it is actually epistemologically, ontologically, cognitively and emotionally invested elsewhere.

Towards the other end of the continuum is to be found that psychologist who feels African psychology should centre Africa in psychology. This is a psychologist who is seized with the desire to articulate precisely that, while there is in certain African countries an African psychology of a kind, it is usually African psychology only in the nominal sense; such African psychology is best characterised as the Western-psychology-in-Africa orientation. Psychologists on this side of the continuum feel that African realities remain marginal within global psychology and psychology as it exists on the African continent. The argument they make is that there is hardly any African psychology, strictly speaking. What this lack calls for, then, is a meaningful and textured Africa in psychology, instead of a nebulous Africa, in order to produce an introverted African psychology – that is, a psychology that develops the greatest number of African publics and makes them its primary audience, readers and users. This model of African psychology is centred on and intended to benefit the greatest possible number of people in the country in which the psychologist works.

These are not pure categories, of course. Both those who look to Europe or the US for inspiration, as well as those who want to immerse themselves in the lived realities in Africa, are not internally homogeneous groups. Psychologists can, sometimes do, change. And they can and do occupy multiple positions simultaneously. Nothing precludes you from being a feminist psychologist inspired by Freud while also being aware of the subjugation of indigenous knowledge.

38 | Invisible Africa

The problem of a nebulous Africa is found in all the sub-disciplines of Euroamerican psychology.

The issue of a master knowledge – and knowledge-making tools – is not confined to psychology and its specialities. A similar problem, to a greater or lesser degree, can be observed in anthropology, economics, gender studies, geography, management studies, political science and sociology. Within psychology, the hegemony of Euroamerican-centrism and its associated master's gaze, ideas and techniques of knowledge-making is more obvious in some branches of the discipline, like psychopathology, assessment and developmental psychology, than in others, like biological psychology.

But it is when we take a look at the less mainstream areas of psychology like community, critical, or cultural psychology that we are confronted with a deep irony: that even those who regard themselves as critics or on the margins of traditional psychology are capable of reproducing an imperialist and colonial architecture of knowledge in their relations with Africa. Thus, the problem of an invisible Africa and the marginality of African thought inheres in the core of the discipline of psychology – indeed, in the very foundations of the social sciences and humanities as a whole. The foundations of psychology, as a discipline rooted in Euroamerican-centred modernity, were built on its opposition to Africa as a primitive object, as lacking, as an absence.

The Nigerian literary scholar and poet Harry Garuba's perceptiveness about the development of silences in the production of disciplines, and how they come to be taken up in Africa, is instructive (Garuba 2012). His insights suggest to me why, in the light of the long process of developing and consolidating the discipline of psychology, a process that began in the nineteenth century, it is necessary to appreciate the role assigned to Africa and Africans. Recognition of the need for an African-centred emancipatory psychology thus begins with an understanding of how Africa and Africans were imagined at the founding of the social sciences and humanities, and still are in these disciplines as we have them today.

39 | Calls to decolonise

In 2015, South African universities rang with loud calls for the decolonisation of higher education. The call is still out: how to design African-centred, decolonised university undergraduate courses, advanced professional programmes and research studies in psychology?

40 | We need to talk

Confusion about decolonisation is as pervasive as that about African-centredness. What is needed is more than just a simple clearing up of this persistent confusion. We are in need of strategies, of innovations. We have to keep going until we completely undo the widespread miseducation about, and deeply buried alienation from, decolonised African-centred psychological knowledge. We need to talk. Learn from each other. Teach one another.

41 | A heterogeneous terrain

Additions to the description of African psychology are called for.

African psychology is not a homogeneous, unchanging terrain. African psychologists disagree about what African psychology is. In fact, some psychologists born and working in Africa do not regard themselves, or are not regarded, as African psychologists. That is really confusing.

Some African psychologists perpetuate knowledge that is prejudiced against Africans. Some African psychologists are conservative, invested in preserving the world in which psychology functions as it is, more or less. And some are radical.

42 | It's power, stupid

I started teaching at a university in late 1996. After years of frustration whose source was sometimes plain but at other times obscured, but a not altogether unhappy decade or so of teaching psychology, I turned away from the discipline. It would be close to a decade later that I finally came to realise fully what has been the real and constant source of frustration – not just my own frustration with the discipline and how it is organised and taught, but the frustration of many students who sit in psychology classes in African universities.

To paraphrase the famous line which is often erroneously attributed to Bill Clinton, the former president of the US: it's power, stupid.

As in any other profession, to be licensed or otherwise recognised as a psychologist is to be legitimated as knowledgeable. Knowledge, in this case, is very clearly the power to define oneself and the world. This is not an original insight.

Psychology is obviously about power – the power to speak as an expert about people's experience and behaviour. This may seem like an original thought, but I have more than a hunch that quite a few anti-establishment, radical and critically minded psychologists have said it already.

Even though it purports to deal with individual behaviour, psychology as it is practised is usually in agreement with the existing structures of power. It counsels people to adapt to their conditions. It teaches students to want to achieve upward mobility within the existing capitalist society.

African-centred psychology is therefore a position taken against the oppressive power of Euroamerican psychology. It is a call to situate Africa at the centre, and not, as is the case now, on the periphery of global psychology. It is an attitude that impels you to place yourself and your world as an African at the centre, to judge the fitness of any theory, approach, or model, every source, technique, or finding, from the perspective of life and time – in a context of severely disrupted histories and multiple temporalities – in Africa. Recognition of yourself as an African-centred psychologist is the beginning of the process of disalienation.

43 | Living with constant resistance

From a certain perspective, in the world in which I travel, through the multiple conversations I have with students, friends, colleagues and university administrators, and having taught and learned from many students, this is what I have come to realise: that talking with others about the benefits of putting Africa at the centre is of the utmost necessity, but to come to consciousness takes taxing self-work, too.

There is no denying it: the debates around African psychology can be a muddle. But more crucially, there has always been resistance to African psychology. And perhaps this will always be the case. There will be institutions that will resist a psychology that puts Africa and Africans at the centre. There will be people who will put up resistance – because of issues of personal power, miseducation, alienation, or for other reasons – even if putting Africa and Africans at the centre of psychology might benefit them or their children.

The simple reason for this resistance could be that a psychology that centres whiteness, Europe, or America is buried deeply in our social institutions. We do not just learn and transmit Euroamerican psychology. Western European and American psychology are in the psyche of African psychologists. And we inject them into our psychology students and patients in turn. If resistance to African psychology is a fact of this knowledge–power complex, we have to find ways to live with it, not necessarily on friendly terms, but with the recognition of its constant presence. We have to acknowledge that even people who are disoriented by Euroamerican psychology, and would benefit from understanding and grounding themselves within a better-situated psychology, can be resistant, because of the inferiority complex generated in them by the hegemonic form of psychology.

95

44 | A psychological history of struggle

You cannot really understand the development of something like modern African psychology without understanding the centuries-long history and struggles of African people. It is hard – no, near impossible – to fully grasp the meaning of the experiences and behaviour of modern African subjects, and the way they live in cities like Lagos, Kampala and Johannesburg – the informality, hybridity and density of life itself – without studying the painful histories of their lives and how they have constantly struggled to overcome adversity and oppression. African-centred psychology is thus compelled to be a psychological history of the lives of Africans.

45 | Healing potential

What original insights are to be gained from African-centred psychology studies about, say, some children's multiple traumas, cognitive development among traumatised children, aggression after a traumatic childhood?

We hardly know, it is true. Very little research exists; that is a fact. And extremely importantly, almost nothing exists in the way of testable explanations – what is often called theory – from African-centred psychological perspectives to illuminate how societies around the world consider embodied heart-and-mind suffering and embodied mind-and-heart healing.

Aspects of Euroamerican-centred therapies, like psycho-analysis and cognitive-behavioural therapy, can and do help some people in Africa. However, having overtly, surreptitiously and unconsciously contributed to colonial rule, coloniality, apartheid and global supremacist white patriarchal capitalism, Euroamerican psychology often achieves more harm that healing. As a result, although we do not have a solid body of African-centred psychology, there is discernible potential for African-centred psychology to become a real positive force. A massive need exists for African-centred psychological work.

46 | Porous hegemony

The need for African-centred psychology arises from, among other things, this fact: decades after the advent of freedom from colonial and apartheid rule, many aspects of the livelihoods, existence and knowledges of the former colonised in African countries continue to be dislocated by the economic, political, social and cultural interests of the US and wealthy Western European nations, specifically the interests of the global capitalist market and the local ruling classes and complicit groups. European and US interests in Africa have a long, devious and rapacious history. Some of these powers are not that hard to identify, but others remain concealed. All of them can be dated to the beginnings of the imperialist and colonial campaigns in Africa in the fifteenth century. The common driving force among all these interests, throughout history, has been the desire to control Africa economically and politically. Everything else follows from and supports this fact.

It is true that even under colonial and apartheid rule there is counter-hegemony. Resistance. Subterfuge. Some of the members of the groups subjected to these powerfully dislocating influences served the interests of their lords. They were, as Freire (2005: 45) put it, 'sub-oppressors' – the local bosses who may be even more exploitative than the original masters were. Freedom among some group members did not mean the creation of a new woman and new man but ascension to the level of new dominator.

It is also true that the dislocation could never be perfect. The hegemony of the dominant interest is never totalising. Among conquered women and men we always see spaces of and struggles for psychological, if not political, freedom.

Of particular concern for a psychology that is seized with the question of the dislocation of Africans is the need to be aware that the interests of the profiteering global and local capitalists, not too dissimilar from exploitative colonial and apartheid interests, want to control how the subjugated people think, what they desire, what they know, and what meanings they give to their experiences. Here too, however, the control is not absolute. There are spaces for resistance.

47 | An offshore model

The received Euroamerican psychology that is taught in African universities was not meant to serve the interests of the majority of the people. It was an offshore, or extraverted, body of knowledge, largely serving the interests of the foreign or local dominant group. The dominance of an offshore model of psychology may be one reason why we have little concerning Africa in psychology. This is the case even though we have large psychology classes, numerous conferences, thriving therapy practices and well-paid psychology professors in universities in countries like South Africa. Sabelo Ndlovu-Gatsheni (2013: 5) has argued that

> one of the strategies that have sustained the hegemony of the Euroamerican-constructed world order is its ability to make African intellectuals and academics socially located in Africa and on the oppressed side to think and speak epistemically and linguistically like the Euroamerican intellectuals and academics on the dominant side. This trap has made it very difficult for African intellectuals and academics to sustain a robust and critical perspective of Euroamerican hegemonic knowledge and the asymmetrical power relations it enables.

48 | Only a situated understanding will do

A question I am sometimes asked is: if we are in Africa, why do we need to build an African psychology (meaning an African-centred psychology)?

It is true that, since colonisation, Africa has become a contradiction. Africa's future – and past – have become entangled with Europe's interests, regardless of whether or not Africans wanted this inconvenient marriage. One example: most African economies trade more with Europe (and then, from a certain moment in history, with the US, and now increasingly with China) than with each other. Another example: most African countries do not have an indigenous language as their only official language.

I have given an answer to this question of why there is a need to build an African psychology. It bears repeating, and if nothing else, this is what is at stake: only a situated understanding can offer an answer to the problems of life as it is actually lived. African psychology is situated psychology. African in African psychology ought to be unspoken, but, because of the hegemony of Euroamerican psychology (even) in Africa, we are forced to say, this is an African-centred perspective on the psychology of (say) leadership, of learning, of children, of cognition, when what we mean is that this is leadership from the perspective of psychology in this situation.

In other words, African psychology is psychology.

49 | Satisfied with alienation

Even though it has become clear to me what is to be gained from building an African-centred psychology, it bears repeating: it is curious that a great many psychologists in Africa have not fully recognised the need to do so. Could I be wrong, and there is nothing to be gained from freeing ourselves from the domination of Euroamerican psychology in Africa? If there is a world to be gained from disalienation, from psychological freedom from colonial, white, Euroamerican-centralising psychology, what to make of this curious state of affairs in which many of us have got lost? How else can we explain a situation in which people seem satisfied with their own alienation?

50 | A worldwide need

There seem to be a number of reasons why the ethical and moral and political and existential duty to contribute to this task of realising an African-centred psychology is obscured. However, there is one major reason that reveals the problem faced by any woman or man in Africa who would call for an African psychology. That reason signals that what holds back the development of African psychology and its potential flourishing is multilayered: it is ontological, it is epistemological, it is political, it is cultural and it is psychical. That reason is the fact that some of us have absorbed the discourse that African psychology may have been necessary for Africans in America, but it was not needed for us, Africans, here at home. There is a pervasive feeling, attitude, or idea, usually unexpressed but one that can be found in action, that 'we are in Africa and do not need an African psychology'.

Not to overstate it: we desperately and totally do. Some of our ancestors may have been captured and enslaved to work the cotton plantations in the Americas, but the slave ideology and colonialism affected even those who escaped the slave ships. Slavery and colonialism stained the whole world, and many black people are still discoloured and disfigured by its long-term effects. We need African psychology for the world, not just for African Americans, and not just for us, here, whose ancestors escaped the slavers' clutches. Even though they sometimes cannot put a name to this need, many African students of psychology, scholars, teachers and practitioners who continue to be privately alienated in their classes, in their writings against the whiteness and Euroamerican nature of psychology in Africa, in their lives, need what African psychology can offer them.

51 | Diverse and dynamic orientations

I suspect some of you reading this might have already said to yourselves, 'Aha, he is essentialising African people. But Africans are heterogeneous.'

I could not agree more. There is no one African psychology that fits all. This is the other factor that has hindered the development of African-centred psychology. There is a view that when I say African psychology, even when I say African-centred psychology, I refer to a singular, static view of African psychology. On the contrary, African psychology is a set of dynamic orientations. African psychology, the way I see it, is best conceived as ways of seeing, to use John Berger's (1972) notion, that are found *within* all of psychology, rather than as a sub-discipline of psychology. Perhaps, though, it is imperative to state that we have to find more than one way to get to the point where African-centring knowledges become a given. Perhaps, then, I have to underline that there are several orientations (to which I will return later on) that constitute African psychology.

52 | Returning to definition

Let us return to definitions so that we can deepen our appreciation of African psychology.

This is one definition you have seen already: African psychology is all psychology out of Africa. This is not altogether wrong. However, it leaves out some significant qualifications. All of psychology in Africa is not for Africa (although African psychology cannot be only for Africa). Much of the psychology work published in Africa is dominated by Western psychology and, in supporting the hegemonic psychological explanations, also bolsters the global hegemony of the US and Europe over Africa. Sometimes this support is given knowingly because the author favours the hegemonic explanations of the world derived from Europe and the US. At other times the support is inadvertent because he or she does not know how to do anything else. And at yet other times, there is pressure to publish, and the author is simply playing the game.

Another definition: African psychology is psychology practised by Africans. Although African psychology cannot but somehow reference Africans, this definition is also incomplete. What of African psychology that emerges out of the US – African psychology practised by African Americans? Inadequate for our purpose.

53 | A psychology from nowhere

Take these two definitions of psychology offered in textbooks. One book was published in the US and the other in South Africa. Looking only at definitions does not give a full picture of the issue, but my intention is to show, rather than tell, why there is a need to situate Africa at the centre of global psychology, why Africa has to be consciously unstated in African psychology, and how best to articulate African psychology. In addition, I think that this exercise enables us to see what African-centred psychology is and what it is not.

In his general introductory US textbook, *Psychology*, John W. Santrock gives this definition: 'psychology is the scientific study of behaviour and mental process' (2000: 5). This definition assumes that psychology, taken as a science like physics, is the same everywhere. But psychology is not like physics. Psychology is a social science. *Psychology* centres the experiences of individuals and groups in the US. I have no objection to this. But let Santrock's book on a US-centric psychology, like many other US textbooks, not be projected as universal psychology. The US is the invisible term in front of *Psychology*.

In *Introduction to Psychology*, which he also edited, Lionel Nicholas (2003a) wrote the first chapter. In the chapter he states: 'While the many definitions of psychology may have varying emphases, all agree that psychology is the scientific study of behaviour' (2003a: 2). This edited textbook, published in South Africa and composed of sixteen chapters, covers the usual major topics of psychology written by authors based in South African institutions: developmental psychology, perception, learning, personality, intelligence, health psychology, and so on (Nicholas 2003b). Nicholas's definition also presupposes that psychology, as the scientific investigation of behaviour, is the same whether you are in South Africa or the American South.

A very interesting feature of the two definitions is their similarity. Santrock and Nicholas are partly in agreement about what psychology studies (behaviour and mental processes) and how it studies its object (scientifically). I wonder, though, if there are any differences between some behaviours and mental processes among South Africans and among US Americans? If there are no differences, of course we do not need African-centred psychology. Euroamerican-centred psychology is all we need.

I think not. Studying humans, as psychology does, is fundamentally different from studying non-humans. Unlike planets, which astrophysicists study, humans never stay discovered. They change their minds. They answer back.

There is something I admire in the book edited by Lionel Nicholas. It appears to take Africa for granted as the place from which the book is written. This, however, is only seemingly so. Nowhere in the introductory chapter is there any consciousness about Africa or any part of it as an unstated location of enunciation. *Introduction to Psychology* apparently presents psychology from nowhere. In this way it is very much like Western psychology textbooks which, while offering a Euroamerican perspective on mental, emotional and relational experiences, pretend to be universal. Of course, it may be that the editor of *Introduction to Psychology* and some of the authors feel Africa has nothing to do with their book. They have every right to feel this way. African psychology is for everybody – including Eurocentric psychologists in Africa.

54 | A proposal

Psychology: A proposal for an introductory textbook by Okon Tleare Pa

Psychology by Okon Tleare Pa will herald a new way of introducing students to the field of psychology. In contrast to books in which Africa is usually non-existent, in this book Africa will be placed at the centre, and you as the student in an African university will also be at the centre. The textbook will be the first of its kind to induct students into the habit of reading psychological research and explanations from an Africa-centred perspective, without presenting Africa as something outside global psychology. While immersing students in psychological theory and studies, the book will teach students how to understand themselves psychologically, not as generic individuals but as persons living in Africa. Students will begin to appreciate their own perspectives on their own and other people's behaviour, thought, emotions and motivation. The book will, of course, cover all the topics covered in most introductory textbooks, but its defining aspect will be how the following topics are introduced and interpreted to students:

Introduction
History of Psychology
Research Methods
Biology and Brain
Sensation and Perception
Consciousness
Learning
Memory
Emotion and Motivation

Language
Cognition
Intelligence
Child, Adolescent and Adult Development
Personality
Psychological Assessment
Psychopathology
Psychological Treatment
Social Psychology
Health Psychology

(What you do not see here is that Africa and its derivatives are the unwritten terms next to each topic: History of Psychology and Africa, African-Centred Perspectives on Consciousness, Personality in African Contexts, African-Centred Psychological Treatment, etcetera.)

55 | (African) American psychology

Some people have said that African psychology was developed by Africans in America. I first came across this notion, stated in this manner, in the 'Foreword' to the book *Handbook of African American Psychology* edited by H.A. Neville, B.M. Tynes and S.O. Utsey (see Cross 2009). The Foreword was written by the African American social psychologist William E. Cross Jr. Cross is known for having developed the psychological nigrescence model of black racial/ethnic identity development. The Cross model of the process of becoming black proposed that the development of black racial/ethnic identity passes through a number of stages in a movement from negative, white normative standards to positive, authentic self-perceptions, namely: pre-encounter, encounter, immersion-emersion, internalisation and internalisation/commitment (Cross 1978; Parham 1989).

About African psychology, Cross has suggested that as a more or less coherent body of knowledge, it has emerged to address the aim of understanding the influences, struggles, conditions, costs and achievements of people of African descent in the US. From this perspective, African psychology arose out of efforts by black American psychologists not only to recognise and produce psychological knowledge that differed from white American psychology, but also – and primarily – to oppose the racist assumptions, theories and research conclusions about black behaviour, feelings and thoughts that are found in this psychology. According to Cross, African psychology was thus not an invention of African psychologists on the continent of Africa, but rather a psychology developed in America by black

American psychologists. Underlining this point, he defines African psychology thus:

> [It is] an invention, a social construction hammered out by Black intellectuals in the Americas – especially the United States. It is a formulation derived from the imagination of Blacks living outside Africa – descendants of slaves lacking direct contact with Africa for over 100 years – who are looking 'back' to Africa for solutions to predicaments, problems, and dilemmas enveloping Blacks throughout the Diaspora and especially the United States. (Cross 2009: xi)

I swallowed it whole. I went on to repeat it. It is not always true, though.

There is much I agree with in these sentiments about what African psychology includes. However, African psychology was not invented by black Americans, however much I admire black American psychologists like Cross, Na'im Akbar, Joseph Baldwin, Kenneth and Mamie Clark, Asa Hilliard, Harriette Pipes MacAdoo, Linda Meyers, Wade Nobles, Thomas Parham and many others. Unless we define much of psychology from Africa as *not* African psychology – which would not only be confusing, but would perpetuate the marginalisation of Africa by some of the people who might identify as being from Africa. In that case, African psychology was born in the US, of course.

This is not to say that there are no connections between African Americans and Africans. The ties are, in my view, inerasable. You merely need to comprehend the history of slavery. African psychologists here and over there have to recognise and strengthen these ties.

However, what Cross and others are really talking about is African American psychology, or African psychology in the US. This is different from African psychology as it appears on the African continent.

Let me repeat once more: all psychology in, about, from, and concerning Africa and Africans, by Africans and non-Africans, is African psychology.

56 | Mischievous questions

In 'What is African psychology the psychology of?' Augustine Nwoye (2015) asks several questions, including the title question, which could be seen as mischievous, as they appear to dismiss decades of substantial work by black scholars in the US on the same question, as well as their efforts to develop African psychology. These questions include:

> What constitutes the major phases in the evolution of African psychology; in what ways can African psychology be defined and conceptualized; what are the principal goals of African psychology; in what ways can African psychology be distinguished from Western psychology; what constitutes the epistemological foundations of African psychology; and what constitutes the subject-matter of African psychology? (2015: 97)

However, what Nwoye may also be understood to be arguing is that the *raison d'être*, status and delineation of African psychology for and within African countries should be considered.

57 | Solutions to alienation

When alienation is the problem, what is the solution? Conscientisation. Self-awareness. Develop your consciousness. Develop your own voice.

58 | Conscientisation

Conscientisation is a fundamental concept in emancipatory African-centred interventions and self-education against Euroamerican-centred psychology. It is a concept closely associated with Freire. Conscientisation, he says, is the means via which 'people, through a true praxis, leave behind the status of objects to assume the status of historical Subjects' (2005: 160). Having become critically aware of being together with others 'in a situation', they will begin the struggle towards humanisation (2005: 109, 119). As an educational approach, it has been absorbed into diverse registers of social activism (including political consciousness-raising). It influenced the strategies of anti-colonial and liberation movements such as the Algerian Front de Libération Nationale, the Frente de Libertação de Moçambique and the Zimbabwe African National Union; its principles and methods can be identified in the ideas of individual political leaders like Thomas Sankara, Amílcar Lopes da Costa Cabral and Oliver Reginald Tambo.

With respect to the struggles to free South Africa from white oppressive rule, conscientising the people through various media, such as radio programmes and reading materials, was one of the strategies for gaining the support of the masses that the African National Congress, the Pan African Congress of Azania and the Black Consciousness Movement in South Africa employed.

Conscientisation can and must be pursued in lecture rooms, in reading groups and through books, if African-centred psychology is to become an ordinary fact. Furthermore, in this age of information, and given the reach of the internet, consciousness-raising work relating to African psychology must also make use of media such as radio, newspapers, television, internet-based tools, apps and all other evolving forms of digital communication.

Conscientisation brings home to you your own alienated expertise and experiences. An awareness of your alienation – including the linguistic alienation of your expertise as well as your experiential alienation – leads to the consciousness that for those psychologists who identify with Africa, a sense of failure will probably persist until there is not only a psychology in Africa, but also a complex and meaningful Africa within the annals and halls of psychology.

59 | A new course

(African-centred) Psychology 101

Welcome to Psychology 101. In this class you will begin the journey towards self-awareness and understanding others psychologically, through an immersion in psychological theory and studies. Most students in South Africa have a vague idea about their own continent and the location of the continent in global psychology. I have designed this course so that you can start to cultivate in yourself what it means to live in Africa and see the world from here. The course will help you to cultivate your consciousness of your own emotions, motivation and thinking. You will learn to analyse your experiences in the world, in your family, among your friends and in your neighbourhood.

While the course covers the common topics of an introductory course in psychology – such as biology, the brain, sensation, perception, research methods in psychology, learning and memory, emotion and motivation, language and cognition, human development, personality, psychological assessment, psychopathology, psychological treatment, social psychology and health psychology – in this class you will be encouraged to critically weigh the topics, studies and theories you will learn about.

Four of the most common questions you will learn to ask are: why was this research considered important; who did the study; how was this conclusion reached; and are there alternative ways to interpret the conclusions? These questions will not only start to develop your ability to think psychologically, but hopefully will also awaken aspects of yourself and the world that you

117

may have taken for granted until now, and contribute towards making you a critical thinker and critical citizen.

The prescribed book for the course is *Psychology* by Okon Tleare Pa.

60 | Complicity

I have not always been fully conscientised to my complicity in perpetuating colonial and apartheid-informed models of knowledge, being in the world, and sociopolitical relations.

It is easier to explain why psychologists who are descended from the side of the colonial and apartheid oppressors may not be conscientised that the lesson they learned at home about what it means to be a white human can be oppressive of black humans. It is not hard to find reasons why psychologists who racially identify as white would be unaware of why apartheid models of knowledge are objectionable. But it is difficult to explain why psychologists descended from the side of the oppressed would not readily grasp that Euroamerican psychology was primarily intended to support the exploitation and control of African countries by the West and its middlemen. Like many psychologists from the ranks of the historically colonised, as a teacher and researcher I have not always admitted that standing in front of a class of students and teaching from a textbook that treats Africa as if it were a footnote always made me complicit in reproducing the dominance of Euroamerican psychology.

You do not have to be an outright collaborator with the enemy to be complicit in the oppression of your self-defined 'own people'. You do not have to be a Lucas Mangope to sell out your people. (Mangope was one of the so-called black leaders of the fake black homeland of Bophuthatswana under the apartheid Bantustan system. The white apartheid government designated Bophuthatswana a republic for the Tswana-language speakers of South Africa. Any Tswana speaker was liable to be forcibly removed from white South Africa after Bophuthatswana had been given 'independence'. Like other fake black homeland leaders, Mangope was more than happy with this fake independence as it made him the president of the fake republic.) You do not have to be an *askari* – the term given to the black turncoats who joined the security apparatus of the apartheid government. A teacher of psychology does not have to actively want to sell oppressive knowledge to black students. And of course there is a difference between those who actively supported the apartheid government as *askaris* and those who were passively complicit with apartheid policy. Nevertheless, the existence of so many highly educated sleepwalkers has meant a long life for Western and apartheid-informed psychology in Africa.

61 | The lost self

It is correct that conscientisation is born out of an awakening to a sense of failure in the face of the continued dominance of offshore models of knowledge and applications within African psychology. I have been a failure. I have been complicit in hawking oppression to black students. How could I have been so blind for so long? How did I think I knew what I was speaking of – please Professor, this way to the podium – when I did not have an authentic voice? It would seem that the struggle to clearly see our situation from an African-centred psychological perspective, the coming to awareness of our failure and collusion with oppression at the very moment we have been promoted and made to feel part of the insiders, comes out of the tussle with our lost selves in an upside-down world.

I n nearly the same words, I have contended that seen from below, from the perspective of the subjugated, exploited, disenfranchised and excluded, read by victims of slavery, colonialism and contemporary global racism, the history of colonial and apartheid psychology, like the history of all knowledge produced by those uncritical of slavery, colonialism and racism, is another reminder of subjugation, of other forms of violence besides the epistemic kind (Ratele 2017b). The ascendancy of Euroamerican psychology, not too dissimilar to the reign of European and American ideas over Africa, always already expresses and celebrates the destruction of indigenous know-how. Western civilisation freights within it the conquest and dehumanisation of what Western discourse refers to as non-Western societies.

Any attempt to write the history of indigenous African psychology is an exercise in trying to produce a history of subjugated knowledge. Like all histories of victims of legislated dehumanisation, be they of the first people, the indigenous, blacks, women, or queers, such a history will always be entangled history: the history of the dominated is trapped, indeed eclipsed, by that of the dominators. It tries to speak of a past outside history, against the existing, readily available colonial archive – which is to say, a library, a museum, a university – reflective of conquest. It seeks to speak to loss, it is haunted by attempts at rediscovery.

Hence, I have said (Ratele 2017b), African psychology will always have a truncated, highly complex history, and a contested, lost, unacknowledged past. Thus, all of it – the past of Africans' psychologies, the beginnings of the history of African psychology, its 'fathers', and how we apprehend the meaning of African psychology – is wide open to contestation.

Where human psychology is taken, colloquially speaking, as the mental make-up of a person or group, it could be said that all human psychology is African psychology, since the origins of modern human beings can be traced to Africa. Given this, but also because it is desirable to be free to talk to all human beings (and animals, plants, other forms of life, and the earth), we have to say that African psychology cannot be restricted to Africa. African psychology might be psychology from Africa – but it is inevitably for the planet.

63 | In and of the world

Let me pose the question: can someone like Jan Christiaan Smuts be considered the father of African psychology? Because, I have suggested, many whites, even after generations of living in Africa, disavow or are excluded from the identity of African. Because African is confounded with blackness. The question of colonialism reappears: the colonialism in knowledge. The question of racism and its racialising effects in the development of disciplines. That is to say, in how racism turns some into whites and others into subordinate races. How are we then to think of fathers of knowledge fields in the context of colonial, racist and sexist domination and exclusion?

In 1895 Jan Christiaan Smuts, a student at Oxford University and later twice prime minister of South Africa, completed a manuscript in which he analysed the personality of American poet Walt Whitman. Considered financially unviable for publication at the time, the manuscript 'Walt Whitman: A study in the evolution of personality' was eventually published in 1973 (Smuts 1973). Could Smuts be seen as the first father of African psychology?

The answer to this question depends on, among other things, what is to be done with the racist roots of psychology in Africa. It depends, given a history in which 'bastard' offspring could be enslaved by their fathers, on how we want to think of white men who fathered African offspring. I am aware that whatever answer is given, it will not be unanimous. But I contend that Smuts did African psychology, if in passing, because of the mere fact that he lived in Africa. As to what kind of African psychology his study of Whitman was, that is a more interesting question.

Nevertheless, here, then, in the picture of the young J.C. Smuts, a student at Oxford with a psychological interest in an American poet, is a sign: psychology students and psychologists from Africa have always been part of the world. They still are.

In addition, psychology students and psychologists from other parts of the world have contributed to African psychology – even if that knowledge was not always for the good of the majority of people of the continent.

64 | Origins of (African) psychology

Psychology in the non-colloquial sense refers to disciplined knowledge. It is the systematic investigation of the psyche. That is one definition. It is not undisputed. Other psychologists prefer to define psychology as the science of behaviour. That is another definition. Not everyone agrees with it. And still others refer to psychology as the study of experience.

All of these definitions – psyche, behaviour, experience – refer to different phenomena. There is actually no universally agreed-upon definition of psychology.

What might be less controversial is the notion that modern disciplinary psychology is found in texts, transmitted through lectures, conferences, journal articles, books, letters, magazines, and, increasingly, virtually through digital media. In that case, if Lionel Nicholas (2014) is to be believed, African psychology born in South Africa can be traced to the late nineteenth century.

65 | Birth of a discipline

You could say, though, that the history of the discipline of psychology is not one of manuscripts, but of university departments, with their lecturers and students. In this light, where the history of psychology is viewed as entailing the establishment of a separate university department, African psychology begins at Stellenbosch University in 1917 with the setting up of the first independent psychology department on the continent.

Having graduated with a PhD with the title 'Zur Erkenntnistheorie Hegels in der Phänomenologie des Geistes' from the University of Berlin in the same year, Reymond (*sic*) William Wilcocks was appointed as the first head of this department.

Could Wilcocks be regarded as the real father of African psychology?

It depends on, among other things, whether someone like Wilcocks considered what he did to be African psychology. And then there is also the question of how he was considered by those who worked with him, those whom he taught, and those who read about him today. No answer is likely to go unchallenged. Again I contend that Wilcocks did indeed do African psychology, because of the mere fact that he lived in and was doing psychology in Africa. As to what kind of African psychology he did, that is a more interesting question.

Regardless, in Wilcocks's studies on Hegel in Berlin we find yet another sign of the reach of the psychology practised by those who live in Africa. It is a psychology that was influenced by German philosophy, and the influence of European epistemologies, values and interests on it persists today. What lies in the future of psychology should be the mutually beneficial influence of African-centred knowledges on European universities and other knowledge institutions.

66 | Paternity claims

A thesis advanced here is that Smuts and Wilcocks are part of the history of African psychology. Depending on the test of paternity, each can lay claim to fathering modern African psychology.

The idea of white males as fathers of African psychology, illegitimate or otherwise, is not one that is going to be readily accepted by some psychologists. Yet both men were citizens of an African country, after all.

Ranged against that claim is the recognition that the two men were of European origin, and that the indigenous Africans were oppressed, their knowledge discounted.

67 | Fatal intimacy

It can seem comic to suggest that African psychology had white fathers. But it also signals the tragic reality: that African psychology in South Africa gets born out of the fatal intimacy between the colonial and the indigenous. And so while one variety of African psychology might inevitably be colonial by birth, it is the mission of another variety of African psychology to resist it, to decolonise it.

All the same, African psychologists, of all creeds, are condemned to live with and work within this entanglement.

68 | Lineage and authority

The genealogy of African psychology can only be contested. The question of this genealogy, which is a question of history, triggers these other questions: who can be part of it? What is it for? Who is it for? But above all, asking about progenitors cues the issue of definition. In relation to knowledge, lineage instantiates authority, and the problematic of what kind of psychology flows from such origins. As such, the spectre of definition cannot but haunt the history, and therefore the future, of African psychology.

69 | Being African

D r Wahbie Long of the University of Cape Town has said that

> [one of the reasons] that the Africanization of psychology in our country has failed revolves around the unhelpful obsession with what it means to be 'African'. More often than not, definitions of 'the African' are framed in racially and culturally exclusive ways that make it difficult for non-blacks to imagine a place for themselves in the field. (2016: 429)

It is *not* incorrect that the interrogation of the definition of African psychology recuperates rows about African identity. Few terms are as generative of heated debate – indeed, of division – in racial and cultural discussions as the term 'African' itself. And this makes sense. For many African women and men, not only fluid, non-binary trans and genderqueer Africans, the term 'African' itself, distinct from matters of gender and sexuality, can be marked by a sense of loss, a sense of being unmoored, of rupture or rootlessness. This sense is often due to the force of slavocratic, colonial, apartheid, military and corrupt regimes which can cut a people from their history. Africanness can be, for some people, bedevilled by feelings of unanchoredness and insecurity.

A preoccupation of a certain African subject who lives in a very modern city like Cape Town, or a city outside of Africa like Los Angeles, is not necessarily with the attractions of a modern life, such as the latest technology or a holiday in an exotic destination like Bali. Instead, Africa as an object of continuous experience can be this person's principal anxiety. The concern is not with how to be modern in contemporary Africa, but with how to be true, how to be faithful, to the fact of being African while being global in your choices, yearnings, uncertainties and exultations.

Is African psychology about Africanising psychology? Some people believe it is. They have every right to their views. However, this is not the African psychology that the disoriented student of psychology in Africa will find meaningful for his or her life. It is not the kind of African psychology that the alienated psychotherapist, white or black, who has encountered only an impoverished lesson, if any at all, about mental life in Africa qua Africa will find readily useful to alleviate the suffering of his or her client.

On the contrary, a tremendous benefit is perceptible in the kind of psychology that does not Africanise American or European psychology but regards itself as an orientation towards the world. Regards itself as one way among several equal ways to understand the life of emotions, mind and behaviours. This African psychology does not adapt (blank) psychology to Africa, where (blank) in this case stands for whichever psychology is meant to be the legitimate version that psychologists and psychology students in Africa are supposed to Africanise, domesticate, modify, or contextualise within the conditions in their countries. This African psychology is a way of doing psychology, a way of seeing the world and Africa from Africa. It is, therefore, a centring of Africans and Africa in the nucleus of psychology. To be at the centre indicates, among several things, a striving to be (an) original, to refuse to be a copy of another, if copying suggests something inferior.

We must note that in an increasingly and more closely interconnected global economy, and with the increasing movement of people across it – without minimising the extent to which such movement is sometimes undertaken at great peril, involving confrontation with nationalistic walls and politics – there is a sense of being copies that we have to embrace. Replication is something that good psychological science strongly encourages, and so should all of psychology in Africa. We are always copying from each other, referencing one another, and not just within science. In everyday life we copy others' views, reference their ideas, use foreign recipes, learn about other places and people. It is hard, maybe impossible, to be entirely original, without some help from others, without building on something built at an earlier point elsewhere by somebody else. The world made possible in the last few decades by electronics, information and communication technologies, and particularly by social media, has made connecting to people in countries we will never be able to afford to visit possible at the touch of a button. Via Facebook, WeChat, Twitter, WhatsApp, LinkedIn, Instagram and other platforms, a person can have friends, followers and other kinds of connections, and belong to groups that include people from all over the world.

There is definitely nothing untoward in learning from others. There is everything wrong, however, in stealing from people, not just by extracting data from them and carting away the resources of their continent, but also by stealing their intellectual labour, their physical labour, and indeed their lands and very bodies to work as slaves, and then denying their contribution to the riches of your country or culture. This is not the place to lay out the history of the enslavement of Africans, the transatlantic slave trade and economic exploitation of Africa. What is being advanced is the argument that copying from each other so as to enhance each other is welcome. What must be strongly rejected is the inferiorisation of some by others, and any further theft of Africa's intellectual and material resources. What African psychology seeks to inject into the thinking of psychology students and teachers and therapists in Africa is precisely admiration of their native talent, creativity, purpose and competency, and of the meaningfulness of their lives.

71 | Four axioms

Four more statements about African psychology (one has to do this again and again until African in African psychology becomes unconscious):

1. All of psychology done in and for Africa is African psychology.
2. All psychological studies by and about Africans are part of African psychology.
3. Both Africans and non-Africans (studying Africans) can do African psychology.
4. African psychology is about Africa and Africans in psychology.

72 | Above all

Above all else, African psychology refers to ways of situating yourself in the field of psychology in relation to and from Africa.

73 | The past in the present

The place from which we come shapes our experience and the self. When the place has been severely disturbed and for a prolonged period, when our experiences of our place and the self in the world have been violently and extensively interrupted, we may get fixated with the place, with its past or future. We may want, for instance, to return so that we can repair the place, and in so doing restitch our experiences and the self. We may desire to go back to make the past better, however irrational the idea of repairing the past appears. We become obsessed with the future of the past, with tradition in the present. Many places in Africa are marked by repeated, sometimes continuous, violent interruptions of experiences and identities. Some Africans who live with these interruptions of experience, with the kind of historical trauma capable of reconfiguring identity, can and do become haunted by the trauma of the past. The past is too much in the present. The question of the past of Africa within modern life thus cannot but be drawn into debates on African knowledge broadly and African psychology more specifically. Yet, while the questions related to what is African about African psychology are almost ineluctable, it would be incorrect to claim that African psychology has failed because it seems to be obsessed with the issues of who is African or with the past. That is to say, that African psychology cannot help us survive modern life, that it is anti-modern (or at best not modern enough). As I have said, African psychology has been around since the nineteenth century and is arguably thriving.

What troubles African psychology, and might make us see failure where there is a complicated history but also well-established African psychology departments, is of course imbricated with the fixation with what it means to be African, and yet it is surely also an aftermath of the lack of clarity regarding what African psychology is. The question of definition is unavoidable. It trips up many. Definitional issues are never fully resolved. African is irretrievably marked by coloniality, an immersive phenomenon. Europe is still in Africa. African psychology exemplifies the profound entanglement of colonial conquest.

74 | Making space for all

Does African psychology refer to studies conducted and healing techniques practised on Africans? Not necessarily. African psychology can study non-Africans. We are obligated to ensure that it does so. It will never be enough to stop at Africans, if it is Euroamerican psychology that shapes how we think about Africa and the world. The world has to be remade in our image, to make space for all of us, if we are to feel at home wherever we might be.

It is true that you come across some academics and practitioners who mistakenly reduce African psychology to a psychology that studies only Africans. However, a vast literature indicates that African psychology is – and must be – the study of all forms of behaviours and relationships, including behaviours of and relationships between non-Africans and Africans, as well as between humans and animals.

An even more crucial point that bears repeating: all of psychology done in and for Africa, by and about Africans, by Africans and non-Africans (working on questions related to Africa and Africans) is African psychology.

75 | Caveat

There is more than one way of situating yourself, of course.

76 | A variegated approach

In my thinking, a number of routes into African psychology exist. One way leads towards the idea of African psychology restricted to Africans. Another begins with but extends beyond Africa and Africans.

The fundamental question posed about Africa and psychology is what frames the meaning and horizon of African psychology. Granted that this is an oversimplification, there are two broad ways to ask questions about African psychology.

The first line of questions focuses on actors, subjects and identities – who is the student, teacher, author, reader, study subject, therapist, or client? In this particular case we might ask the question: is African psychology a psychology that focuses on Africans? Some researchers, teachers and therapists may be inclined towards an African psychology of this kind. However, such an approach could also limit the potential and future of African psychology as a global enterprise. That is to say, when such identity-related questions are used to frame African psychology, African psychology often appears as an esoteric branch of psychology, perhaps even an area of work outside of psychology. It is on the basis of such identitarian questions that African psychology gets to be defined as *studies and therapies (of X, whatever X is) on or for (and sometimes, although slightly different, by) Africans.* All the same, although there are researchers, teachers and therapists who may prefer African psychology thus defined, it is but one way to conceive of the work.

The second line of questions concerns standpoints, methods and applications – what the topics of interest are, how to approach them, and what interpretations can be derived from the data. From this angle we might ask: how might we undertake research or see therapeutic work from an African psychological perspective? This places African psychology within psychology, even if in an oppositional stance towards the mainstream. Such a question seems to lead towards a more variegated African psychology. The definition suggested by these questions is this: African psychology refers to *ways of situating oneself in the field of psychology in relation to and from Africa.*

77 | The ultimate goal

Why should there be an African psychology if African psychology is not necessarily a psychology that studies Africans?

In simple terms, the main stimulus for an African psychology was to get out from under a Euroamerican-centred psychology dominated by the rich Western countries, which have been led since the Second World War by the US. In South Africa, the struggle was against apartheid psychology.

The ultimate goal in searching for an African psychology has been to build a relevant, appropriate, sociopolitically conscious, transformed or decolonised discipline and profession. The search for an African psychology was sometimes explicitly labelled as such, but as often was barely traceable under various discourses such as relevance, appropriateness, or transformation.

Of course, there is no one-to-one correspondence between something like a decolonised psychology and an African psychology. Some African psychological research can be colonialist, racist and sexist. What is needed is not only to centre Africa in psychology, but also to develop an African-centred psychological register that is conceivable as part of a relatively long intellectual history of de-Westernisation, to contextualise, transform, or decolonise psychology and, more generally, knowledge in former colonies and the global south.

78 | Real constraints

Is the name 'African psychology' not constraining?

Of course the name 'African psychology' has real constraints. But remember that the term 'African' in African psychology is supposed to be silent.

The limitations of a term like 'African psychology' include how, more than a label like 'US psychology' or 'South African psychology', this term can burnish stereotypes of Africa as a special case. African psychology is not a special psychology. There is a very clear need to have something called 'African psychology'. Sometimes. It is a psychology that seeks to speak in its own name. A psychology from a part of the world that has been historically excluded in thinking about the world. A part of the world that finds it ludicrous that hypotheses, explanations and tools of a psychology meant for Western Europeans or Americans dominate African countries. 'Sometimes' points to the fact that it is often necessary for those who do psychology on the peripheries of the world, particularly when they have to communicate with and orient those at the centres of the world of psychology, to retain labels like 'African', 'Chinese', or 'Latin American psychology'. As such, the label 'African psychology' is usually retained for the sake of charting the entangled world that needs to be described, and pointing out to the powerful centre how realities out here, in this corner of the universe in which we live, are actually different from those at the centre.

The limitations of the label 'African psychology' are therefore very real, and not easily overcome. And, when they are overcome, they keep returning, even when we would like to be known simply as psychologists.

79 | Debates and contests

There are two crucial and specific limitations of the label 'African psychology' that are worth accentuating.

First, unless your desire is to contort yourself like a circus freak, all psychology regarding Africa and Africans on the continent and in the diaspora has to be counted in the body of what is seen as African psychology. This seems a straightforward characterisation – except when it is not.

Second, the problem with the name 'African psychology' arises from the fact that debates about African psychology reference, usually implicitly, other debates about histories of slavery, colonialism and racism. African psychology partakes in existential, ontological and political contests such as those about who can be African, and whose home is Africa, besides those issues of who can teach about Africa, who is entitled to teach Africans, and who can do psychological repair work among Africans. An implication of all these broad and specific contests and debates is that it is hard for African psychology not to be political, even when it wishes to remain neutral, as these issues derive from the politics in African countries.

80 | A contingent term

The unstated question is: why is there a need to use the adjective *African* psychology instead of simply taking all psychology done in Africa on Africans and non-Africans as psychology, period? What some scholars seek to do with the term 'African' is to distinguish between different ways of thinking about Africa, being African, and psychology. Arising out of this quest, again usually implied rather than explicitly stated, are to be found attempts to differentiate between psychology that *identifies with* or empathetically *centres* Africa, and a neutral psychology that approaches Africa as one object among others. As such, while all psychology that is taught, studied, published and applied in South Africa, just as in other African countries, is of course African psychology, the effort has been to surface psychology teaching, research and applications that consciously identify themselves with Africa. The latter is what is sometimes referred to as African-centred/Afrocentric psychology. Wade Nobles has this to say about this distinction:

> We, therefore, should not be just talking about psychology in Africa. To simply bring Western psychology to Africa is to be complicit in the mental brainwashing and psychic terrorism . . . of Africa and the adoption of the very tool and theories that have been used to demean, defame, debilitate, and damage us. In effect to merely advance Western psychology into Africa would be akin to uncritically drinking poison as if it were medicine to heal and revive ourselves. (2015: 402–403)

Even when the distinction has been made clear, the questions we pose about Africa, Africans, the West and psychology will tend to close down or open up how we think of an African psychology. Thus it is necessary to recognise that the term 'African psychology' is contingent, can have multiple meanings, and, in countries like South Africa, is overladen with the political history of colonialism and apartheid racism. The term 'African psychology' will therefore have to be always contingently embraced by students, teachers, researchers and therapists, even as psychological work from different countries of Africa remains in need of strengthening – in some countries, like The Gambia and Equatorial Guinea for instance, considerably more so than in others. Strengthening African psychology is a gargantuan task. This task includes the need for psychologists moved by the ideal of a more just world to keep these three ideas in mind: taking up the challenge to redefine the relation between psychology and Africa; vigorously and sophisticatedly locating Africa in global psychology; constantly highlighting the situatedness of all psychological knowledge and practice.

81 | Polyvocality

I have referred to the idea of African psychology as situated knowledge practice; a practice tied to the knowledge maker's or user's situatedness or orientation. What does it mean to say African psychology is situated knowledge and practice?

Situated African knowledge and practice is work that is conscious of its birth, history, context and point of view. Situatedness signals location, position, orientation, or standpoint. To be situated begins with appreciating your biography, sociality, perspective and interpretations. African psychology, seen in this light, is the same thing as situated psychology. But situated psychology is not always African. US psychology is situated psychology, as are British, Chinese, French, Islamic and Latin American psychology. All psychology is situated. However, the fact is that in a world differentiated by economic, military, racial and cultural power, on average those who have better access to such power have little need to situate their knowledge and practice; that is, little need to acknowledge their situatedness.

What is called African psychology is not a separate body of knowledge but a way to *situate your work* and *yourself*. But people situate themselves in different ways in any field of knowledge and practice. As situated practice and knowledge, African psychology is not one single thing but a polyvocal and dynamic enterprise. It is made up of different voices. It is not static. In that way, African psychology is composed of different orientations. And how you are situated in or oriented to the world frames the research questions you ask; presents the world to you from a certain perspective and occludes other possibilities; influences your therapeutic goals, success and failures; determines what you teach and what you leave out.

82 | Four orientations

Having come this far, I would now like to give an outline of my framework for (thinking about and doing and seeing) African psychology as situated knowledge and practice. Better yet, of understanding African psychology as a set of orientations. Whereas we can be forgiven for thinking of African psychology as all of psychology in Africa, about Africans, by Africans and non-Africans, the distinguishing and anchoring element of the framework is precisely this: African psychology is a set of repertoires tied to how we orient our studies, teaching and therapeutics to individuals in Africa, and, equally important, how we orient ourselves to the world from places in Africa. African psychology is, therefore, situated knowledge and practice.

The main idea underpinning the framework is this: African psychology is composed of multiple orientations towards Africa and psychology. There are four orientations, distinguishable from each other by how you situate yourself with respect to psychology and Africa, to Africa in psychology (Ratele 2017a). The number of orientations is not definitive; the fact that there are several orientations is what matters.

The four orientations that constitute African psychology are:

1. Euroamerican or Western-oriented African psychology;
2. psychological African studies;
3. value-based, spiritual, metaphysical, philosophical, or cultural African psychology (cultural African psychology for short); and
4. structural, materialist, political, or critical African psychology (critical African psychology for short).

In Figure 1, I offer a diagrammatic representation of these four orientations.

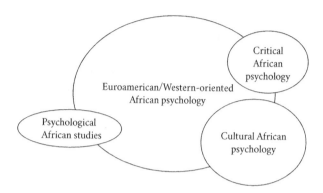

Figure 1: Four orientations in African psychology

Some of these orientations are readily graspable – such as the more Western-oriented psychology in Africa. As the mainstream, this Western-oriented African psychology is where the majority of psychologists are situated, and the literature produced from this orientation is too vast to reference. The other three orientations are represented by a handful of scholars (Mkhize 2004; Nwoye 2015; Semenya & Mokwena 2012).

83 | Notes on Western-oriented African psychology

Western- or Euroamerican-oriented African psychology considers African psychology as the study of behaviour (in African settings). This is an orientation (stance, position, perspective) towards Western Europe and the US which occupies the mainstream of psychology in South Africa. It is deeply influenced by a feeling, sometimes a belief, maybe a clearly spelled-out view or one that is implicit, that Western psychology is by definition psychology. Not African psychology – that is something else.

Western-oriented African psychology makes up the core content and concepts of what is taught in universities, the therapeutic modalities used in consulting rooms and psychiatric hospitals, and the research work that is published in journals and books. We are taught to accept the psychology topics and approaches and tools and interpretations and psychotherapeutic modalities coming from Canada, France, the United Kingdom, and a great deal more so from the US. And these are the things that we who are teachers teach our students. We come to believe that work from Somalia and Surinam, or Cameroon, Chile and China, is not quite psychology. We certainly struggle to think of those who have not qualified as doctors of psychology or psychotherapists as professionals able to help in alleviating psychological pain, or to explain the meaning of happiness (unless they belong in a fashionable category, like monks).

A Western-oriented African psychology stance assumes, implicitly or explicitly, that psychology is an undivided science. Some who subscribe to this stance believe that psychology is a science in the way that astronomy and chemistry are sciences – that is to say, that it is ever apolitical and value-neutral. But psychology is informed by politics and values in a way that natural scientists can never grasp. Many psychologists also fail to grasp the value-laden nature of their discipline. Or maybe they refuse to face up to the reality that humans are not stars, and societies are not chemicals.

Under what conditions would you consider a thesis, say a master's or doctoral study, as excellent that quotes only or mainly authors from Western Europe or North America?

I read many master's and doctoral theses in my areas of interests. Some I read so as to keep abreast of what students and young researchers are doing in the field. Others because I am asked to examine them. Many of these are adequate. In fact, I could say that many of these dissertations are more than just satisfactory when compared to some of the works I have read from universities outside Africa. But because of the colonial inferiorisation of intellectual work coming from Africa, both teachers and students often fail to recognise the warped and alienating standards they have set for themselves.

The inferiorisation of much of the intellectual thought produced in Africa is internalised by blacks and whites in Africa alike. We find here, then, an instantiation of what Harry Triandis (1994) was referring to: the fact that many psychology students and psychologists in Africa have an inferiority complex vis-à-vis American and Western European psychology. Dissertations are considered good merely because they quote all the 'right sources', and thus are associated with some amorphous external standard set in the West.

Sometimes, however, the standard is very well defined: you have to read this researcher or that theorist, and nearly ten times out of ten it is someone coming from Europe or America – John Bowlby or Burrhus Frederic Skinner, Stanley Milgram or Melanie Klein, Abraham Maslow or Max Wertheimer; you cannot not read this theory, explanation, or model and be passed.

The crucial point is not that these theorists do not have anything worthwhile to say about conditions in Africa. It is not to argue that there is nothing to learn from explanations about psychological life developed in Europe and America. It is, rather, that the idea of the West is being elevated to the standard against which we measure the excellence of the work itself. To repeat what I said earlier: we have to overcome these pervasive and debilitating inferiority complexes.

It is on this terrain that you come upon a terrifically thought-provoking problematic. Some of the master's and doctoral work I read is really superb. Such work is acutely exciting to consider, precisely because these dissertations are technically superior, and they therefore trigger questions about how we measure excellence in context.

An instructive example should help to make the point. In 2017 a doctoral thesis was sent to me to examine by the Department of Psychology at the University of Cape Town (UCT). Titled 'A critical analysis of men's constructions of paying for sex: Doing gender, doing race in the interview context', the thesis, focused on South African men, was highly accomplished. The word 'critical' in the title was well considered, and not an attempt to appear smart. In spite of a few weaknesses, the researcher produced a fine piece of scholarship. Written by Monique Huysamen, a white Afrikaner feminist woman, the study was admirably embedded in the literature. The candidate was obviously well read in high theory, drawing on names such as Judith Butler and Michel Foucault, and employing approaches and tools such as feminist poststructuralism, intersectionality, discourse analysis and performativity.

The proficient analysis and critique offered by this doctoral student was one that appeared to be deeply uncritical of its subjection to Western European and US critical thought. It was a critique moulded by what I have referred to as a Western or Euroamerican psychological orientation. She was superb, then, in the world as it is – not as it could be. She was oriented, in her approach and interpretations (although not in regard to her site and participants), towards the West.

The electrifying question for me is, therefore, how does one judge a superb Western-oriented psychology doctoral or master's thesis produced in an African university like UCT, or any of our universities, even while recognising that it leaves the world as it is?

The point is this: to say that Western or Euroamerican psychology as taught in African universities was not, and is not, intended to bring the majority of those who would study in these universities closer to their collective real interest, does not mean a doctoral study that is grounded in Euroamerican-centred interpretations is by virtue of that fact a weak study. The real concern of the majority of those who study psychology at African universities like UCT, especially those who would claim labels for their work such as 'social-justice-oriented', 'anarchist', 'liberatory', 'feminist', or 'radical', is to recognise, among other things, the evil of injustice, to challenge unearned privileges, to rage against corruption, to work for freedom wherever there is oppression, to resist coloniality.

Some would, of course, disagree with the claim that a study grounded in Euroamerican-centred interpretations is not weakened by that fact. We can see why this disagreement needs to be aired. A study that reproduces the hegemony of Euroamerican thought restates the intellectual subjugation of African-centred thought to the West. A critical doctoral thesis conducted in an African university that fails to be critical of its reliance on

Euroamerican theory could be said to echo, even if unwittingly, the notion that little originality worth that name comes out of Africa.

The trouble with this critique, though, is that it also recasts the world as one made up of good guys and bad guys, in a black-and-white universe. America is bad, Africa is good. Africans are innocents, Westerners are evil. Obviously, this is untrue. In the postcolony we cannot afford to gloss over the reality of entanglement. We have to reckon with the real possibility that we may never achieve complete decolonisation in our subjective lives, lecture rooms and scholarship. Therefore, even while we strive for a world as it could be, a world in which we are reflected in our fullness, that decolonised world is not yet fully born, and we live and teach and research for change in the world as it is.

In the end, though, Africa has to be centred in our analyses and critiques.

* * *

Monique Huysamen responds:

'In short, I agree with you in entirety.

'I keep returning to your words: Afrikaner. Feminist. Woman. This is the first time anyone has used the term "Afrikaner" to name me, in conversation with me. I feel put in my place and out of place. Being positioned as a white Afrikaner, it feels, has set decolonial thought up as something already out of my reach.

'I don't think I defined my work in terms of decoloniality while I was writing up my PhD at the University of Cape Town. Perhaps everyone should write about the thinking that happens in the months after submitting a PhD. A year since finishing my thesis I have moved to the United Kingdom, starting a research assistant job at a traditional psychology department there. In this space I unapologetically define

myself as a decolonial feminist scholar, and I do so with a sense of resentment towards the discipline of psychology. I find myself writing about whether psychology as a discipline that has gained its legitimacy and currency through maintaining and perpetuating the denigration of the black Other can be compatible with decoloniality at all. Perhaps my feeling that I both want to and can express a strong identification with decoloniality as an academic in the UK has something to do with the fact that here I am confronted with my "Africanness", or at least being "from Africa", in a way that is different to when I am at home. Having been a white student in South Africa meant that I have had the luxury of never having had to prove my academic worth in spite of my Africanness. But in England I have had to take basic English language tests to prove I can speak English – despite it being my native tongue and the language I dream in – simply because I am from Africa and I hold "only" an African PhD. In UK academia I am regularly confronted with small reminders of the systematic inferiorisation of African scholars and of African intellectual work by the global north in a way that my whiteness had largely sheltered me from before.

'Perhaps what stunned me most when I moved to a psychology department in the UK was the realisation that psychology undergraduate and postgraduate students in South Africa seemed to be better equipped to engage in debates and questions that are complex, nuanced, and critical than their counterparts in psychology departments in the global north. Certainly when it comes to the kinds of critical research areas I am interested in, South Africa appears to be producing stronger psychology students. My suspicion seems to be confirmed by your reflections on having examined PhD theses from both inside and outside of Africa. But the important question here is why had I been so surprised (almost disappointed) that psychology students from my own country might produce work that is more nuanced and complex than those educated in the global north? I have internalised this inferiorisation of African scholarship. My surprise reflects exactly these

159

warped and alienating standards that we as African scholars set up for ourselves that you speak of. I expected South African scholars could be "as good" as those from the global north, but somehow hadn't imagined them as being better.

'The question of citation you raise is an instructive one. Sara Ahmed (2017) (again writing from outside of Africa, further driving home your point) unapologetically states that she follows a strict citation policy: She does not cite white men, she cites only feminists of colour who have contributed to dismantling the institutions of patriarchal whiteness. After reading Ahmed's thoughts around the function of citations both as a means of acknowledging our debts to those who came before us, and as the building blocks for academic and institutional homes we inhabit, I subjected my thesis to the same questions you have raised here. A look at my list of citations begs the question, where are the African voices? These voices aren't completely absent from my thesis as you suggest they are. They certainly are there, but they are in their usual place – at the margins. As long as theses produced in Africa, such as my own, are deemed "excellent" and are not held accountable by academics, such as yourself, for their failure to make central and build upon African knowledge, we will, whether we like it or not, continue to contribute to the colonial project of keeping African knowledge at the margins. We will continue to feed our own inferiority complexes.*

'How does it happen that a PhD written by a student such as myself who cares about feminist politics, who cares about queer politics, who cares about anti-racism and decoloniality could produce a PhD that marginalises African knowledge in this way? Because South African academia as an institution continues to systematically produce students like myself. (The silences in the syllabus of course remain important in this production of students. I completed a social work degree and my psychology degrees in South Africa over ten years and in that time, with my particular combination of subjects and courses,*

I did not once learn about Steve Biko at university. Did you know that I read the beautiful work of Manganyi for the first time a few weeks ago [after graduating with a PhD in psychology]? This certainly speaks to my own complacency as a white academic, but I can assure you I did not have to learn about Le Bon and Freud outside of the curriculum.) This inferiority complex you speak of has been methodically ingrained in us. This importance of looking to the global north, of proving ourselves "as good", has been embedded into every step of our educational training; it has been infused into our very making as young academics. We were taught, time and time again, the importance of showing that we can link and align our research to that which is produced in the global north. We need to read and cite these theorists in order to pass: to pass our degrees yes, but more importantly to pass as "real" academics. We are taught to produce our work for the global north. Perhaps South African universities will find that they will begin to produce more PhDs that position African knowledge and theory at their centres when students no longer have to write them knowing that two out of the three examiners will be "international" and inevitably be situated in the global north. Perhaps when students are systematically taught to look "over here" rather than "over there", taught to produce knowledge not only about Africa but for Africa, encouraged to work specially towards building and growing African intellectual thought, we can start to set our sights upon more honest questions of decolonising higher education and the kind of thought that it produces. So as I said, in short, I agree with you in entirety.'

85 | Notes on psychological African studies

Africa, it is true, tends to be a shadowy figure in mainstream global psychology, and for this reason if nothing else I have to be part of a resurgent project to centralise Africa in all areas of psychology in Africa. In my pursuit of this goal, Africa and the many meanings it attracts from foe and friend – some colonial, pejorative, racist, stereotypical, others nativist or mythological, and still others emancipatory, but always dense and elusive – are central figurations in my attempts to understand boys, men and masculinities (in Africa and elsewhere). I have to appreciate that Africa has been tremendously affected by the wars – armed, structural, cultural and symbolic – waged on its ordinary people by European and US imperialists, colonialists, home-grown dictators, army generals and capitalists. I am therefore keen to understand Africa *itself* as an actor, a dynamic entity on its own, an object of interest, and a place of knowledge-making, that needs thinking about within all studies, teaching and psycho-therapy. In my case it means that in thinking about men and women and other genders, I have to think about them from where I am located and where they are positioned in a place in Africa. Psychological African studies as an orientation emerges from the need to use psychological tools to understand subjects as positioned in a world within Africa. As one of the four orientations within African psychology, psychological African studies at the basic level is primarily a transdisciplinary orien-tation towards Africa, Africans and psychology. In that sense it also has one foot in Western psychology and another in African studies. However, whereas Western psychology is defined as the study of individual behaviour, African studies refers to those studies whose object is Africa. Psychological African studies thus is defined as psychology aimed at integrating the theories, tools and insights of psychology, including tools from psychoanalysis, in order to study Africa (Ratele 2017a).

Psychological African studies includes tools from psychoanalysis. An appreciation of the potential contribution and development of psychological and psychoanalytical African studies begins with an understanding that psychology or psychoanalysis was never one of the core disciplines in African studies. Colonial, missionary anthropology formed a tendentious nucleus of the first generation of African studies curricula which sought to 'build an understanding of Africans and the African world in an elaborate but misguided exercise at seeking to know the "native" Other who was defined from the outset as being "tribal" and, therefore, fundamentally different and consigned to the lower rungs of the ladder of human progress' (Olukoshi 2012: 26). The anthropological stereotypes of Africans in early African studies courses were part of what motivated Kwame Nkrumah, the first president of Ghana, to exhort scholars of Africa he met in Ghana in 1962 to move from anthropology to sociology (Garuba 2012). Thus, after the Second World War, when the call to end colonial domination gathered momentum, scholars in the fields of history, economics, politics, culture, languages and religion, in addition to radical and anti-colonial African and Africanist scholars in the disciplines of anthropology and sociology, began to question and rewrite the study of Africa that had been taught in European and US universities (Olukoshi 2012).

The fact that psychology did not form part of African studies programmes does not imply that psychology was not among the disciplines that regarded Africa and Africans as backward and in need of European civilisation or, since the

Cold War era in the US, in need of Western-led development. It also does not suggest that psychology has made strides towards decolonising itself so as to understand Africans from their own perspectives, and for themselves, instead of understanding them as the Other.

It is perhaps necessary to point out again that even though everything produced and undertaken by psychologists in Africa must be recognised as African psychology, there is in fact very little of what is referred to as psychologically inclined African studies. Still, even while psychological African studies does not yet exist as a coherent enterprise within African psychology, it is a potentially exciting growth area for African psychology as well as for global psychology. Of course, there are psychologists in Africa and elsewhere whose work reveals a non-colonising interest in Africa as an object of study (for example, Cooper 2013; Nobles 2015; Nsamenang 1995), and who have laid some groundwork for this enterprise. There is also existing work by non-psychologists that uses psychological or psychoanalytic concepts upon which this project of psychological and psycho-analytic African studies could be established (for example, Biko 1987; Fanon 1963, 1970; Mbembe 2001, 2003). Although his main concern is how postcolonial thought in the work of people like Biko may be useable to transcend the increasing orthodoxy of much of critical psychology, Hook (2005) gives an indication of how we might appropriate a range of existing theoretical resources in psychology to study Africa.

Orienting African psychology as part of African studies means using psychological and psychoanalytical methods, theo-ries, tools and insights *within* African studies. Psychological African studies puts psychological processes at the centre of its enquiries, and yet may not necessarily put the individual, as conceived of in much of psychology, at the centre of the world.

This form of African psychology would borrow from the theories of psychology, but probably, if it is going to feel at home in African studies, would learn to take seriously non-psychological studies of societies, histories, politics, cultures, languages and religions in Africa. Such learning would have to entail African psychologists engaging in dialogue with the works of African writers of literature. There are so many: there is Chinua Achebe, Chimamanda Ngozi Adichie, Ayi Kwei Armah, Mariama Bâ, J.M. Coetzee, Teju Cole, Tsitsi Dangarembga, Unity Dow, Nawal El Saadawi, Buchi Emecheta and Nadine Gordimer; there is Bessie Head, Alex La Guma, Naguib Mahfouz, Kopano Matlwa, Zakes Mda, Thando Mgqolozana, Nthikeng Mohlele, Helen Oyeyemi, Wole Soyinka and Ngũgĩ wa Thiong'o; and there are many more. This means that the work of some African psychologists working from this stance, the work that dialogues with these and many other writers, is boundless.

Additionally, scholars and teachers in other disciplines like African history, African politics, African philosophy, African art, and increasingly African gender studies, will be unavoidable interlocutors. The development of psychological African studies, therefore, will lead to it becoming a recognisable body of knowledge within African studies if psychologists read and interact with those writers, scholars and teachers in disciplines which have gone further than psychology in developing a body of knowledge in studies of Africa. African psychologists working within the framework of African studies would have to enter into dialogue with African scholarly, literary and other creative work outside of psychology.

There are several challenges in the way of developing African psychology as psychological studies of Africa, and here are two. First, the development of psychological African studies can be hampered by, and has to overcome, the fact that disciplines *come with* and often *are* the theories and tools. This applies to all the humanities and social sciences: the disciplines teach how to understand the world. Much of Western psychology, in particular, sees the world as comprised of essentially separate individuals. Even social psychology is fundamentally directed towards studying the individual in society. Is it possible, then, for a discipline that is founded on the idea of people as primarily individuals to conceive of people as primarily part of the others with whom they live, as some cultures are wont to do? To enable the development of a situated psychological African studies, there would be a need to unlearn *some* of the ways in which the discipline of psychology understands people.

African psychology as part of African studies can further be inhibited, as suggested earlier, by the perception that African studies tends to be dominated by historical, political, economic, sociological, cultural studies and literary perspectives. The implication here is that African studies can be experienced by psychologists as inhospitable to the insights and tools of psychoanalysis and psychology. And because such scholars are already not abundant within African studies, it means that those psychologists who dare to work from this position may have to work hard to develop dialogues with other Africans and Africanists about how to make the claim for the importance of understanding the working of the psyche in the study of Africa.

86 | A note on cultural African psychology

The third orientation of African psychology, the more culturally, spiritually, religiously, metaphysically, philosophically inclined African psychology, situates the investigator and the investigated, the therapist and the client, the teacher and the student in a cultural world. This psychology also believes in spirits, in non-material entities such as God and ancestors, in other invisible dimensions that interact with this one. For the sake of convenience we have given the name *cultural African psychology* to this orientation; it is not a perfect name. As it concerns itself with values and beliefs and traditions and spirits and the supernatural, we can also refer to it as *value-based psychology*. Cultural or value-based African psychology begins by placing people in their cultural context, seeing practices from the people's cultural point of view. Philosophies of life, world views, life-worlds, cultures, traditions, beliefs, or values are placed at the centre of this psychology. The cultural effects of colonialism and apartheid racism are also seen as figuring prominently in the lives of Africans. The object of study is the person in their cultural, traditional, spiritual, or religious context, and the values and beliefs that shape the person. The problems of the person seeking counselling are seen to emerge from the dynamic between culture and person. An understanding of the culture is as important as an understanding of the person. The student who comes to the psychology class is seen as a cultural being, bringing his or her culture into the lecture room.

87 | Traditions and modernities

I am struck by the understanding that we cannot fully grasp, on a large scale and in granular detail, the development of African modernities without first appreciating the challenges and hold of the past, of history and traditions. We will find it hard, for example, to understand how some people speak of their experience of modern African cities such as Lagos and Luanda, in contrast to how they speak of their experience of traditional life, without first understanding the store many people set by cultures and traditions while also struggling to have those cultures and traditions respond to their contemporary needs in African urban spaces.

What can you do with cultural African psychology? From a certain angle, values are at the heart of the science of human behaviour. Perhaps all human activity is always about values. If this is so, then value-based African psychology enables what no other kind of psychology has been able to do – that is, understanding human beings as value-driven. To study psychology from this orientation would be to study how people are driven by, make, contest and change values.

To illustrate the potential of cultural African psychology, consider most events we might read of in newspapers or witness in daily life. Whether it is in relation to the uplifting acts by Orlando Pirates soccer players Kermit Erasmus and Daine Klate in walking onto the pitch with their kids to collect their Nedbank Cup medals and trophy, or Boko Haram's abduction of more than two hundred girls in Chibok, Nigeria, or the trial of the athlete Oscar Pistorius for fatally shooting his girlfriend, Reeva Steenkamp, the question of how cultures are organised, what humans value, or what we believe about a range of phenomena is always in play. In the above examples, we see how footballers interact with their children (in a way that has become more widely acceptable only in recent decades, and was not commonplace in previous generations); how terrorists relate to girls and young women (abducting them and forcing them into marriage); how some men relate to their intimate partners (and the violence that attends such relationships). What connects these examples is the subject of men and masculinity, and some of the associations of masculinity with cultural beliefs and values. What research investigations from the vantage point of, and courses in, value-based African psychology might be able to offer in these instances are insights into the conditions that facilitate involved fatherhood among footballers; the prevalent kinds of relational norms and perceptions of girls and women among terrorists; and contradictions in enactments of, and discourses on, values on violence and love in intimate partnerships.

This is a well-known fact, but it might be useful to repeat it here: a culture that leaves emotional nurturance of children to women tends to be one in which men are left – leave themselves – to do the soccer playing, thinking, fighting, earning and politics. There will be girls and women in such a culture who fight to play soccer, do thought-work, go to war, provide economically for themselves and their families, and politically represent their society or groups in that society. There will be men who desire and fight to be involved in looking after children, dislike violence, and believe females make as good or bad politicians as males and they deserve an equal chance to fail or succeed. The watchword is fight. Anti-patriarchal women have to set themselves against the cultural hegemony in a patriarchy. Men who prefer egalitarian relationships with women in a patriarchal culture are by definition non-hegemonic. In South Africa, we continue to privilege patriarchal values in our schooling and university education system, at times habitually and at others deliberately. More specifically, hegemonic patriarchal values are conveyed in psychology courses in universities, alongside theories of child development, learning, stress and psychopathology. The transmission of male domination is neither intentional nor malicious, we might say – ignoring precisely the fact that hegemony implies consent. However well-intentioned patriarchal norming in university education broadly and psychology classes specifically may be, it does not make the systemic cultural diminution of women and girls any less real. The values without which the domination of men over women becomes difficult do not work alone. They intersect with capitalist values, and white supremacist values, and values regarding the earth and its resources. In a society in which democratic close relationships between women and men are not as valued and ubiquitous as male-controlled ones, and these undemocratic relationship norms are mutually reinforced by other norms that support authoritarian social relations, it is no surprise that our basic, further and tertiary education systems (alongside the media and family, the key vehicles for shaping a culture on a wide scale) continue to reproduce a certain way of being in the world. This is the system to which many parents hand over their children, boys and girls, black and white, to be educated.

Consider this example. A few years ago an interesting and illustrative debate took place in the public sphere about why even parents of black children hand over their children to be educated in this system. It is a great example because it shows the complexity and intersections of culture, race and gender in politics and education. The journalist and historian R.W. Johnson claimed that blacks are keen for their children to attend schools which were reserved for whites under apartheid because these schools offer quality education (Johnson 2014). The article in which this claim appeared was a comment on the short-lived appointment of Mamphela Ramphele, the leader of the Agang SA political party, as the presidential candidate for the Democratic Alliance (DA) political party.

In Johnson's view, the mistake was that the white female DA leader Helen Zille was trying to 'anoint' the black female Ramphele as her successor. It is now much clearer that the near-fatal political error was made not by Zille, but by Ramphele in accepting and then reneging on Zille's jobs-for-pals offer. That seems to have turned many potential voters away from Agang.

In Johnson's appraisal, all of these political miscalculations are cut from the same cloth as other white–black relations. 'One notes how African, Coloured and Indian parents are eager,' Johnson (2014) wrote, 'that their children should attend formerly white schools – it is seen as a guarantee of quality – and also how, for the same reason, they do not want the whites to abandon the school to them: the ideal is to be racially diverse and keep the whites involved.'

He received strong criticism for his crypto-racist, patriarchal views. Talk-show host and essayist Eusebius McKaiser asked him, during one of his radio shows, whether Johnson had come up with that argument while drinking brandy and Coke with his friends, or if there was any peer-reviewed support for the claim (McKaiser 2014). What we must be most critical of is the belief underpinning Johnson's racist arguments about quality education. This belief is shown by his uncritical employment of the four-races model that was at the centre of apartheid laws. The idea that South Africa was made up of four naturally occurring, rather than socially engineered, races – indeed, the idea of using race to differentiate and govern humans – is one many of us still hold on to, in spite of all the evidence that race is a social, not a biological, construct. This is politically, culturally, economically, psychologically and scientifically very problematic. Nevertheless, like many other people, Johnson casually writes about race categorisation as if it were a law of nature, when in fact these categories were fabricated by apartheid ideologues who classified people into four races: Africans, coloureds, Indians and whites. South Africans are no longer supposed to be officially classified in terms of race groups. However, the post-apartheid government reveals its ambivalence about the four-race groupings, as it still asks people to classify themselves in terms of these race groups, and produces many official reports on the state of the nation and development in terms of these and additional categories like 'Other'. Even though it is politically righteous to remain cognisant of the history of the domination of those who accepted their classification as whites over those classified as black, we must never cease to be critical of the roots of the idea of race in Euroamerican colonial racist consciousness. The most important function of the idea of race has been and continues to be racial segregation. All forms of racial segregation (all structures, projects, policies and cognitions that overtly or covertly support racial separation) invite the notion of biological supremacy of some humans over others.

While this must remain a hypothesis until it is empirically tested, let us suppose that there are African, coloured and Indian parents who hold that historically black schools are not as good as schools in formerly white neighbourhoods, and feel that their children will receive better-quality education at previously white schools.

There are at least two groups that are lumped together in this argument.

The first group consists of those African, coloured and Indian parents who, because of where they live, send their children to historically white schools in their neighbourhood. It is necessary to consider this group of parents, who live in or close to historically well-resourced, previously white-designated areas, in our reflections about changes in education in the post-apartheid era, and about the schools where children whom Johnson and many of us continue to designate as African, coloured and Indian might end up. Where else would these parents have their children attend school? In the old, under-resourced, racially segregated neighbourhood?

The group that Johnson seems to have in mind, however, consists of those African, coloured and Indian parents who may still live in previously segregated so-called non-white enclaves but send their children to schools in historically white areas. The false assumption made by Johnson is that these parents choose without restrictions to send their kids to historically white schools because these are better schools. This is not necessarily the case.

So why do they choose to send their kids to these formerly white schools? Is it simply, as seems to be suggested, that these parents are eager to be associated with whiteness because white means quality? I think there is a clutch of factors – such as the possibility that the calibre of teachers who teach in historically coloured, African and Indian schools remains comparatively low, that these schools have non-optimal class sizes, poor infrastructure, frequent interruptions related to teacher protests or community-related ones, non-delivery of textbooks, and outbreaks of violence around and within the schools, alongside the relative performance of historically disadvantaged schools compared to historically white ones in terms of examination results – which persuade black parents who can do so to avoid some of the black schools.

In short, the choice parents make to send their kids to formerly white schools is not made without reservations. Parents are making the best of a sorry situation. In the kind of society in which we live, black parents who are living in townships or rural areas and can make such choices are faced with a dilemma: send your child to a nearby historically black school where the chances of getting a good Grade 12 pass may be lower, or ship them off to a historically white school where their chances of feeling like outsiders are higher.

Of course, the government must accept responsibility for the larger part of the failure to radically improve conditions in schools so that black parents are not forced to decide between such disheartening options. Yet, as black people we must shoulder some of the responsibility for ignoring cultural struggles in basic, further and tertiary education. It is time to get together and build more independent and community schools – a space which has been taken by commercial interests. Schools developed by progressive black individuals, churches and communities are not unknown in black global history. Community schools make sense when the children coming from the community are excluded from the good public schools or cannot afford the fees in private schools. Community schools make sense when the community wants to take charge of the education of the children in the community. Independent education need not be expensive or elitist. If new, independent, quality schools are founded by black people, while progressive forces and politically conscious individuals continue to engage with government to speed up the improvement of conditions in historically black public schools, the need to send black kids to historically white schools will decrease, and the pressure on schools in historically black neighbourhoods will be reduced.

Here is something to bear in mind, though. Making our schools produce final exam results with one hundred per cent 'bachelor passes' (that is, passes that meet university entrance requirements) is only part of the picture. It is a grave error, one for which we will always pay a price, to continue to define quality only in terms of high percentages in the final school year results. And the same holds true for university education.

Where quality is defined only in terms of school grades, without taking into account the need to educate young people towards developing the qualities as a person that we envision – what we refer to as values, or what in another era were called virtues, such as reciprocity, kindness, respect for others, respect for the earth, generosity, equality, sharing and non-violence, and of course non-sexism and non-racism – there is an argument to be made in favour of historically white schools. In that case, let's have more black children going to formerly white schools. It makes perfect sense, if passing the matric exam with distinctions (the highest grades) is my primary criterion for quality education, to choose for my child a school where he is likely to achieve distinctions. I can convince myself that the distress I experience about the fact that the school population is largely white in composition will have to wait for another day. But would this be wise?

Quality education ought to contribute to quality of life. There is some evidence regarding the relationship between these two things. But what needs ongoing critical reflection is what – given the anti-black history of colonial and apartheid education – quality in this case entails. How, for instance, does a quality education whose hidden objective is to alienate us from our cultures, even if that alienating education results in a big, beautiful, white house, square up with quality of life? What is the worth of an education whose outcomes are multitudes of individuals estranged from the deepest yearnings of the self, an education that internally divides identity, leading to the constant, disorienting sensation of an individual living as if she were looking at herself from the outside? A sensible, disalienating quality education is fundamentally informed by an imagining of the future we want to have. The price we will always pay in handing over boys and girls to schools and universities that teach them to admire white, Euroamerican-centred values, often subtly conveyed in any single lecture or lesson but cumulatively destructive over the long term, is high. The costs of doing so include alienation, but also meaninglessness and purposelessness.

In the long run, the rewards of having black children receive education in historically white schools appear to be ambiguous, in that the education they receive there is embedded in the very ideologies, norms and values which reproduce the cultural subordination of blacks, and allied consequences of this. Clearly, this calls on us to reconsider how we can move beyond the curious phenomenon of educating black children into racially alienating cultural traditions in a post-apartheid society. There is a place, clearly, for teachers, researchers and therapists educated in cultural African psychology.

As a parent of a boy, I would not want him to be an academic superstar and yet oppressive to others and filled with hatred for himself. I do not want a school that teaches my child that black cultures are inferior to white cultures, that girls have fewer rights than boys, or that homosexuality is a sin.

I suspect that most parents – black, but also white – assume that giving our children a good shot at the world through a quality education means helping them to achieve a good pass in high school, and get a good university education. More than that, though, I suspect most parents harbour the hope that our children will turn out to be virtuous men and women.

This is a false hope, and a false assumption.

89 | A note on critical African psychology

With a more materialist, political, or critical orientation, African psychology seeks to be attentive to the materiality or structures of daily life, including economic and political and other social institutions and structures. This is what I refer to as *critical African psychology*. As it concerns itself with structures that govern our lives, including our cognitive and emotional lives, another name we can give to this critical African psychological orientation is *structural psychology*. According to this stance, these institutions and structures are seen as shaping psychology, and a critical African psychology perceives itself as oppositionally situated, within yet against economic, political and other structures. Like the previous two orientations, critically oriented African psychology tends to be interdisciplinary and transdisciplinary, appropriating its theories and methods from critical and radical African thought, critical Western psychology, and critical and radical Western thought more generally. Critical and structurally inclined African psychologists prefer to pose questions about the workings of power and knowledge in societies, institutions, groups, relationships and within psychology. This orientation is distinguished from cultural African psychology by its suspicious stance not only towards US and Western European psychology, but also towards all psychology and notions of culture.

What kind of critical (or feminist or Marxist or other type of oppositional) psychologists are they who work in Africa, but think of critical psychology as fundamentally opposed to African psychology? This is the question I was confronted with when I re-read an article by three highly regarded African critical psychologists, Desmond Painter, Peace Kiguwa and Werner Böhmke. In 2013, Painter and his colleagues published a well-written article, 'Contexts and continuities of critique: Reflections on the current state of critical psychology in South Africa' in the journal *Annual Review of Critical Psychology*. I say 're-read', because I had read the article once before, prior to realising what the problem was that they were not seeing. And, of course, an African-centred consciousness about how a Euroamerican-centred world makes us dizzy about our situatedness in Africa takes time to develop.

In their article, Painter, Kiguwa and Böhmke are very critical of African psychology because, among other things, they rightly say, it does not question 'its status as – and desire to be – psychology' (Painter et al. 2013: 856). When African critical psychologists like Painter, Kiguwa and Böhmke are critical of African psychology because it does not question its desire to be psychology, they are not being critical of all of African psychology, only of a certain orientation. They are not being critical of a Euroamerican psychological orientation in Africa. They are not being critical of psychological and psychoanalytical African psychology. They are not being critical of critical or structural African psychology. They are being critical of value-based or cultural African psychology. This is what makes them oppose African psychology as a whole to critical psychology, and produce a sometimes curiously Africa-blind critical psychology.

This is what the three scholars say in their article:

> Although there is certainly common cause to be found between the African psychology movement and critical psychology more generally, the former maintains a complex relationship with both mainstream and critical psychology in South Africa. On the one hand it is clearly a form of critical psychology: it critiques and rejects (much of) the ontological assumptions and value systems it perceives to be at the core of 'Western' psychology, and seeks instead to found its psychology on a different, uniquely *African* metaphysics . . . On the other hand African psychology departs from critical psychology by not always questioning its status as – and desire to be – *psychology*. Adherents of the idea of an African psychology often do not wish to break with the academic and professional project of psychology (and the cultural force of 'psychologisation'), but on the contrary to take ownership, through 'Africanisation', of the institutional positions and professional rewards that psychology and being a psychologist still make available in postcolonial South Africa, but that had been largely inaccessible to black professionals and intellectuals during the colonial and apartheid era. In other words, an uncritical valorisation of 'culture' may arguably function as a strategy of class distinction and mobility, which – if the notion of the 'African' itself is never interrogated critically – may not just mystify class interests, but bolster emerging discourses of an exclusionary African nationalism . . . (2013: 855–856)

There is convergence between myself and these three colleagues about the alliance between critical psychology (by which I think they imply Euroamerican-centred critical psychology) and African-centred psychology as a whole. However, there is a major weakness in their argument about what they refer to as African psychology. Like many others, critical and uncritical, conservative and anarchist, they misperceive their object. They are confused, and may be confusing their students.

The confusion is threefold. First, they see African psychology as one unified thing. They refer to it as a movement. But African psychology is composed of multiple perspectives. It has many voices. It is a position within broader psychology. Second, if there is one idea that is *always* interrogated by many African people, it is the meaning of African. Third, for some really curious reason they seem not to see themselves as African psychologists although, as far as I know, they were born and work in African universities. I am not sure how they manage to do this. In my view, they are African psychologists, and the question for them to ask themselves is how they are positioned in relation to (critical) psychology and Africa.

＊　＊　＊

About my claim that 'they are not being critical of all of African psychology, only of a certain orientation. They are not being critical of a Euroamerican psychological orientation in Africa. They are not being critical of psychological and psychoanalytical African psychology. They are not being critical of critical or structural African psychology. They are being critical of value-based or cultural African psychology', Peace Kiguwa replies:

'I think that we are – that is, critical of African Psychology [AP] as it is currently conceptualised in all of its entirety. An orientation

developed out of an African cosmology as the cornerstone of AP is not the disputed issue. In fact, it is a desired objective. The issue at hand is the unquestioned belief in and working toward something that we call "psychology". The belief that we can "do a better psychology" (in the form of AP). The current decolonisation calls in psychology suffer this assumption – that psychology remains a discipline, practice that is needed.

'Critical psychology suffers this misleading orientation as well but perhaps fares better in its fundamental raison d'être – never taking psychology as a given.'

About African psychology as a 'movement':

'This remains useful [as] a description to my mind. Much like the Decolonisation movement – that also comes with multiple faces and meanings of decolonisation – there is a need to describe the socio-political, economic, symbolic climate that influences the current calls for Africanisation.

'"Movement" is used in a sense of capturing a mood/moment/ climate. Having said this, there is still an epistemological problem at the heart of AP.'

About the meaning of African as always interrogated by many African people:

'Perhaps, but I do not always see this interrogation reflected in much writing on AP. If anything, this interrogation of what it means to be African remains caught up in immutable and static notions of "Africanness". The fluidity, the relative-dialogical nature of how this identity can no longer be spoken of in purist terms is not often present in much of the writings. Maybe we need a hybrid for how we do psychology?'

About not looking at oneself as an African psychologist:

'Speaking for me . . . if I had to frame myself (and take some ownership of the category of psychology) I would certainly describe myself primarily as a critical psychologist doing work that is centred *on and for Africa. Many a psychologist works (and perhaps [was] even born) in African universities but does decidedly anti-African work. Geographical location therefore cannot be a criterion for how we name ourselves.*

'My reticence in claiming as my overarching frame the category of "African psychologist" is the possibility that I will adopt precisely the blinders that I seek to continuously interrogate in my work.

'My reading and appropriation of a critical psychological frame (though I am aware that the blinders can and do exist here as well) is that I am able to stand outside of psychology as discipline and practice. That is a position that remains important for how we persist in doing psychology.'

What distinguishes the various African psychological orientations shown in Figure 1 (Section 82) from each other is the manner in which two central ideas – Africa and psychology – are apprehended in each of them, although the way in which the two ideas are approached often remains implicit. The most significant element present in all of them, however, is that we, psychologists and students of psychology, are always situated, unconsciously or after deliberation. The four African psychologies can therefore be considered as ways in which actors are positioned in relation to Africa as an object of study, to psychology's place in Africa, to Africa as a place of knowledge-making, as well as to their own being, social relations, perspectives and expertise. The crucial point is that orientation, or situatedness – that is, the way clinicians, counsellors, teachers of psychology and researchers are positioned or position themselves – has an effect on psychotherapy, counselling, teaching and research.

The different African psychological orientations presented in Figure 1 are not meant to correspond to the established branches or areas of psychology such as critical psychology, cultural psychology, cross-cultural psychology, political psychology, economic psychology, or indigenous psychology. They are also not meant to correspond to established sub-disciplines of psychology such as general, cognitive, developmental, personality, community and social psychology; nor to the categories of professional registration such as clinical, counselling, industrial, educational, research, neuropsychology and forensic psychology; nor to the divisions of the professional associations of psychologists. Instead, these different African psychological orientations are, in my assessment, found *within* the areas of work, *within* sub-disciplines, *within* registration categories, and *within* the divisions of the professional association. In South Africa, some areas of work, sub-disciplines, registration categories and divisions will evidence more debates on African psychology than others, simply because of the numbers involved.

It is worth noting that African psychology teachers, researchers and psychotherapists can and do move across these different orientations. The boundaries between the four psychologies are permeable. It is likely that individual psychologists will at different points in time orient themselves in one way or another with regard to Africa and psychology.

To observe that psychology in Africa has been influenced by Euroamerican presuppositions, notions and morals is not an argument for a Euroamerican-centred psychology in Africa. Of course not. I am against precisely the wholesale importation of Euroamerican-centric ideologies, explanations, ways of seeing, values, norms and ways of being, conveyed in psychology, and their imposition upon the ways of living of the Others of white, capitalist, middle-class America and Western Europe.

At the same time, to argue against a psychology that centres Euroamerican presuppositions and ways of living in itself – although these may be thinly concealed by questions, theories, models and approaches that claim to be universal while privileging Western European and American ways of knowing, being, and relating to others – is not to be interpreted as a call to expunge all foreign ideas from African psychology. This would be an impossible task. Euroamericanism is in us. And some of its ideas are definitely worth keeping. Augustine Nwoye (2017: 44) has contended that 'although some Eurocentric theories of the human personality or personhood . . . already exist, including those developed by some African American psychologists . . . some of which are very relevant to our experience, a continental African version of the theory of African human personhood is still needed'.

All psychologists in African countries, but in particular Africa-centring psychologists, ought to assert their right to, and avail themselves of, the European archive. It is common knowledge that Africa's encounter with Europe from the fifteenth century onwards forever changed both continents. Additionally, European civilisation contains property and ideas stolen from Africa and the New World. Most significant for African psychology, however, is the pronounced need for more interchanges, and more openness to influencing each other, across African countries. In this respect, mobility between different countries and exchanges among continental psychology students, researchers, teachers and therapists are necessary. Beyond such intra-African exchanges, African psychologists need to interact with African psychologists in the diaspora. And African psychologists must produce psychology for the world, not only for Africa.

93 | Continued hopes and frustrations

In May 1970 Noel Chabani Manganyi published a paper on hysteria among mainly African women in the *South African Medical Journal* (Manganyi 1970). In the same year he completed a doctorate in psychology at the University of South Africa (Manganyi 2013: 281). Depending on whether you accept or reject the idea of white men like Smuts and Wilcocks in Africa as African (taking into account that some of them may have been race supremacists and anti-black), Manganyi could be seen as the rightful father of African psychology, and the history of African psychology as beginning circa 1970. Knowledge produced by black scholars in psychology and other disciplines is indispensable. A need to draw out the ties and crossings between African psychology and black studies (as well as other fields such as African studies and cultural studies) also exists. But there is, in my estimation, a perennial danger of African psychology being conflated with psychology by black scholars. Even worse, African psychology can be relegated to studies on black people by black psychologists. Psychology by black scholars is linked, but not identical, to African psychology. African psychology is a much broader enterprise. Above all, African psychology is not a discipline.

Since Manganyi began his work, there have emerged a number of radical and conservative black scholars in psychology. Black psychology students and psychologists have called for a relevant, appropriate, non-Euroamerican-centred psychology for South Africa. In recent times, the call has become more insistent, and the debates more intense. It is true that these debates have also been characterised by prejudice, knee-jerk reactions, nastiness and apparent frustration. Despite that, the debates about African psychology, along with the demands for decolonisation and free education for university students, and the establishment of the Forum for African Psychology as a formal division of the Psychological Society of South Africa, have, as a call for papers in *Psychology in Society* stated, 'reignited some of the old hopes and frustrations about psychology' (Psychology in Society 2016: 1). The intensifying call for a transformed, decolonised, or African psychology ought not to be ignored. In my assessment that is what prevails: it is as if there is a hope that this demand for African psychology will go away, later if not sooner. As noted in the call for papers, 'among some teachers of psychology, therapists, researchers and students, the term African psychology continues to conjure ideas of a psychology not simply different from American psychology, but of knowledge that is not real psychology' (2016: 1). These ideas arise from a deeply mistaken understanding of African psychology.

I must repeat what I said earlier: like Manganyi, Reymond William Wilcocks was an African psychologist. Not a black psychologist; but, being a psychologist in Africa, an African psychologist. So the inspiration for the call for an issue on African psychology was

that whilst some unenthusiastic reactions are evident, the renewed calls for African-centred psychological thought and practice offer an opportunity for critical psychologists to think about their own suspicion of and alienation from Africa, the hegemony of concepts mainly born out of conditions in US and Western Europe, what might African studies contribute to critical psychology and vice versa, while continuing to contribute to global knowledge. And although the old question about a psychology in Africa without Africa

in psychology still cries out for radical and sophisti-
cated resolution, new problems have begun to press on
us within critical psychology. (2016: 1)

The 'opportunity for critical psychologists to think about their
own suspicion of and alienation from Africa' was not taken up as
enthusiastically as we had hoped. What we were looking for, but
never managed to find, were contributions that would speak to
'how critical psychology might give birth to decolonised, transformed and African-situated conceptualisations, analyses, and
insights without losing sight of global concerns that characterise
psychology' (2016: 1).

94 | (African) developmental psychology

Take any branch of psychology – let's say, human development. As with all of psychology, the foundational problem
in the psychology of human development is that of an absent,
nebulous and dark Africa, and of strange or stereotypical
Africans. The problem reaches far beyond developmental
psychology, beyond psychology actually.

Given the realisation that the problem of so-called dark
Africa or a nebulous Africa in psychology extends beyond the
branch of psychology of human development, let us nevertheless ask a few questions of developmental psychology. These
secondary questions are not intended to point an accusatory
finger at those psychologists who identify as developmental
psychologists. If there is any accusation whatsoever, it is
directed to ourselves, and concerns what we have ignored or
accepted to make ourselves comfortable within the university and professional establishment, content to reproduce the
master's grand psychological narrative.

Here, then, are two paradigmatic questions that we have
to keep in mind when educating ourselves, or others, into an
African-centred orientation. The first question, directed at the
most general level of our alienation, is why we stick with developmental psychology, despite its birth in or domination by US
and Western European psychology, but more importantly why
we continue to use its models, when we can see that the socioeconomic conditions under which children develop in many
cultures in Africa make many of the models of child development
in Euroamerican developmental psychology suspect, sometimes
injurious. Do we really believe that the responses of an American
white middle-class male undergraduate (a favourite subject

191

in psychology research in the US) to questions about human development are transferable to males (and females) in places in Africa, that they are adequate for an understanding of psychological development in Africa? If there is a suspicion that there are gaps in our knowledge, or that there is a mismatch between the Euroamerican developmental psychology taught in university departments in Africa and people's actual development, why have we not been conscientised into or energetic in creating a developmental psychology with Africa at the centre?

Just in case there is any confusion about my question, let me say clearly that Euroamerican developmental psychology is exactly that: it centres European and US realities. It asks about child, adolescent or adult development in the US or Western Europe. It might pose as a study of all humans. But a close examination of studies of human development coming from the US and Western Europe shows that the standard, the centre, what is considered normal, is really a value. That value is Euroamerican.

The second question is directed towards a more specific issue. Imagine that you were asked to write a textbook on developmental psychology for undergraduates. What would such a textbook, one that is less extraverted than the standard Euroamerican-centred textbooks, look like? Would it be odd to have chapters with titles that include mention of Africa, or of specific countries like Nigeria, Niger and Namibia? It is common, that is to say, to find African scholars mentioning Africa in the titles of their books, chapters, or journal articles. While not a negative in itself when mention of the place of study is required, what this tends to communicate, or what African scholars are forced to state, is that the work is provincial, concerned only with Africa, not universal.

We ought to ask: if we take Africa for granted in an African psychology, what would such a book usher forth? We ought to ask: if we take working from an Africa-centred position as an unstated given, what would a study, one for the world, look like? These are the studies and books we need, informed by an African-centred orientation, meant for the world seen from Africa.

Where African-centred psychology is seen not as a sub-discipline of psychology but as an orientation towards Africa/Africans and the field of psychology, African-centred developmental psychology is to be found in the *interstices* of African psychology and Euroamerican-centric developmental psychology. I see African-centred developmental psychology lying not between Western developmental psychology and African psychology, but within African psychology and in relation to Western developmental psychology as they currently exist. African-centred developmental psychology is a psychology of human development that situates Africa at the centre. An African-centred psychology of human development that tries to marry approaches, frameworks and precepts from Western developmental psychology and African psychology might be worth trying out. But my preference is for us to develop ways of seeing (in this case, for instance, how children acquire social skills or how we age well); to relearn to look at biological, cognitive, or sexual development from the perspective of our interactions and situatedness in Africa, rather than roughly joining Euroamerican-centred and African-centred views of human development.

African-centred developmental psychology is developmental psychology that not only challenges US-produced explanations about child and adult development in African families, for instance, but also conscientises African developmental psychologists against 'extraverted, alienated and dependent' (Hountondji 1990: 9) expertise.

African-centred developmental psychology challenges African psychologists and US psychologists in the area of human development to be more critical of their own thought and practice as psychologists.

Of course, African-centred developmental psychology that looks to the conditions, the thinking about, and the feeling for life and social structures in African countries for its ontologies, politics, epistemologies, methodologies, publics and technologies of living, is still in the making.

We have to have discussions about the misrecognition of Africa and Africans, the ethnocentrism, blind spots and gaps in Euroamerican developmental psychology; but also about the overlaps (wherever they are) and tensions, contradictions as well as similarities (where these exist), between that developmental psychology and African psychology that could lead towards an African-centred developmental psychology.

95 | (African) community psychology

O r let us take community psychology. We can begin with a quick look at two textbooks on community psychology published in South Africa. They offer eye-opening lessons on this matter. The first book, *Community Psychology in South Africa* (second edition, published in 2012), is edited by Maretha Visser and Anne-Gloria Moleko. The second book, published in 2001, is *Community Psychology: Theory, Method, and Practice*. The editor is Mohamed Seedat, with Norman Duncan and Sandy Lazarus as consulting editors.

The textbook edited by Visser and Moleko has nineteen chapters covering topics such as mental health, HIV/Aids, different theoretical approaches, social support, crime and violence, substance abuse, poverty and inequality, race and intergroup relations. An intriguing aspect of this book, which declares itself to be embedded *in South Africa*, is that one of the chapters, written by Boshadi Semenya and Makgathi Mokwena (2012), seems to be aimed at presenting a more African take on community psychology. This is confused and confusing thinking. Imagine that the book was called *Community Psychology in ~~South~~ Africa*. South Africa is a country in Africa. To have a chapter on Africa in a book on Africa is muddled thinking. But it is also forced on many of us by the entanglement and contradictions caused by settler colonialism and apartheid that provoked a sense of South Africa as not African, or not-quite African. It may also be that the chapter falls into the trap of thinking of Africans primarily or only as defined by the religiously 'cosmological', of Africans as essentially mythological and spiritual in their reasoning. The chapter in question has the title 'African cosmology, psychology and community'. What is eye-opening is that in this book written by South African authors and published in South Africa, the chapter by Semenya and Mokwena seems to be the only one expressly intended to give an 'African' perspective. In contra-distinction to this, the rest of the book expresses an uncertain view as to whether it is African or not, or, more precisely, what kind of African it is. I contend that the mere fact of this book being edited and written by authors from Africa and published in an African country makes it a book on (African) community psychology. But of course it does not make it African-centred.

Community Psychology: Theory, Method, and Practice also has nineteen chapters. But Seedat's compilation is a different kind of text from that edited by Visser and Moleko. It may be because Seedat's book is pitched at a more advanced level, and so is able to introduce complexity in ways that Visser and Moleko's collection does not. The most telling aspect of this book is, however, the inclusion of a section called 'Perspectives from elsewhere'. This section includes a chapter titled 'Community-based community psychology: Perspectives from Australia', by Brian John Bishop and his colleagues, as well as another chapter titled 'Community mental health in the USA: Challenges to urban community mental health centres', by Elisabeth Sparks. What is intriguing about this section is that it makes all community psychology, including that from the US and Australia, *perspectival*. While it situates itself in South Africa – and whether this contextualisation is executed successfully or not, meaning without othering itself, is debat-able – it does gesture towards the existence of other contexts in which community psychology is produced and practised. The book in fact has an additional subtitle, *South African and Other Perspectives*. As in the case of Visser and Moleko's volume, the fact that *Community Psychology: Theory, Method, and Practice: South African and Other Perspectives* is edited and written by authors from Africa and published in an African country makes it a book on community-centred African psychology. Is Seedat's volume African-centred, though? That is the question.

While more open to other community psychologies than other branches of psychology, global community psychology is numerically – which in itself is not a problem – and ideologically – which is a problem – dominated by US-based community psychologists. South Africa has a flourishing community psychology fraternity. However, African-centred community psychology does not exist. That kind of community psychology lies in the *interstices* of African psychology and (US) community psychology.

As part of an ongoing effort to develop a situated, emancipatory, African-centred psychology, socially conscious psychologists in Africa need to raise the problematic of a master community psychology as it is taken up in places in Africa, juxtaposing it to the possibilities of an African-centred psychology focused on communities.

I would like to reiterate that African-centred community psychology does not lie *between* (US) community psychology and African psychology but in the *crevices* of African psychology and (US) community psychology as they currently exist. I have suggested that African-centred community work that tries to marry community psychologies from different contexts might be an interesting approach. However, because I see African-centredness as a stance, thinking into existence a community psychology that situates Africa at the centre would be best.

Looked at from another direction, African-centred community psychology is an African psychology that locates itself in the community. African psychology is to be found within community psychology. Community psychology must be located with African psychology.

Someone says, 'Moving to New York gave me a whole new perspective on the world.' What does she mean?

Or, at some point in your life, you may have said something like, 'Johannesburg [or whatever place you have moved to] opened my eyes.' What did you mean?

I say, *becoming fully conscious* to what it means to be you, to be *awake* to what it entails to be of African descent, to *recognise* yourself as black, to be white and born in Africa, or to be of a kind of heterogeneous heritage and identify with Africa, is what fundamentally shifts your understanding of the world, whether you are in Johannesburg or New York.

I say, taking time to learn how you are made to see the world, and then cultivating your own way of seeing the world, regardless of where you find yourself, is what opens your eyes.

The need to understand the existential significance of having Africa at the centre applies to cognitive psychology, to psychopathology, to social psychology, to neuropsychology; it applies to health psychology, political psychology, feminist psychology, positive psychology, psychology of men, work and organisational psychology; it applies to all of psychology.

It has never been clearer why we need to understand the importance of African-centredness, but also how immense the task is of weaning ourselves from Euroamerican-centrism.

To disalienate ourselves we have to come up with not just ideas, but methods, models, behavioural tests, therapies, explanations and technologies in African-centred psychology. We have to find and create ways of conducting work and teaching informed by such a psychology in the African communities or groups of interest to us. We have to contribute towards a framework for being in, engaging with, understanding and writing Africa as the default in psychology teaching, research and theory-making. We have to conscientise ourselves towards being disenchanted with any kind of psychological knowledge and practice that does not centre Africa.

African-centredness in psychology begins and ends with a number of tenets.

It is focused on social relationships – of Africa and Africans to psychology. It is inspired by the interactions and identities it is motivated to study, and by the desire to make these understood by the interactants (persons interacting) and identities in question.

Within the university it aims to raise the social consciousness of students and it is open to learning from students.

In the field of research, an African-centred psychological investigator, beginning with the questions she poses, and having made and explained her findings, would want to empower those who had participated in her studies and would become further educated by the knowledge of the participants.

African-centred psychology would liberate us, the psychologists, from the European and US 'authorities' in the discipline and our lives.

Above everything else, African-centred psychology would fully embed itself in the realities of Africa, its histories and traditions, economies and cultures, politics, religions, multiple temporalities and modernities, even though it must always be looking at and responding to the world at large.

98 | Psychological freedom

Freedom, even as apparently straightforward a type as political freedom, is not that simple to grasp. Freedom from what? Freedom to do what? Does political freedom simply mean the release from oppression, to vote, stand for office, freely participate in politics? Or does it always signal and require other types of freedoms? Can we have political freedom when we do not have freedom to express ourselves, to associate freely, where the media is inhibited? What does it mean to be politically free but without a decent job? When you sometimes go hungry? In a starkly economically or sexually unequal society? How much sense does it make to say that the group to which you belong – say, men as a group, or whites, or heterosexuals – is free when other groups are oppressed by, or on behalf of, your group? These questions are vital for anyone interested in political African psychology; in teaching about political emancipation; in tracing the history of African freedom struggles; in looking at the future of freedom. In a book about looking at the world from a certain place in that world, though, we can limit ourselves to considering concrete acts of freedom to make freedom apprehensible. Freedom *from* the overt or subtle coercion to see the environment, self, and others in a way that privileges a white, male, Euroamerican gaze is cardinal. The individual's autonomy *to* look is a sine qua non of political freedom. And, absolutely, freedom always calls for other rights.

It is axiomatic that white racism seeks to turn black people into inferior humans. It wants to render them as servants. It criminalises them. It infantilises. Or, when it wants to be charitable, it stereotypes them as pitiable creatures.

The same holds for sexism: its goal is to turn women into objects, into bodies, into childlike beings who look up to men, or into men's helpers. The effect, in all cases, is to subordinate them to men.

The same is also true of how the rich look upon those who are poor. The poor are lazy. They are delinquents. They are pathological, harbouring mental and medical diseases. They have to be felt sorry for.

To understand how to overcome oppressive systems such as white racism and sexist patriarchy, the stereotypes they convey and their effects, do we not want to know how these systems achieve feelings of inferiorisation in the very subjects they oppress? How they are able to introject feelings of being lesser beings in those they target?

It is true, as far as I can see, that like the gluttonous capitalism under which we live, white racism aims to perpetuate the enslavement of the black psyche. But how did this psychical disfiguration become possible? Via which routes? Why did we allow these inferiorities, objectifications, revulsions, exoticisms, hates and fetishes into our hearts and minds? What are the routes to black self-belief, black authority, black self-care, black love and black authenticity in a whitened world? How do we then become psychologically free of racism, of sexism, of homophobia, of xenophobia, or of exploitative capitalism, if indeed we can?

If political freedom is an involved idea, when it comes to psychological freedom we step into an infinitely involved world of human emotions, cognitions, behaviour and relations.

Defining freedom as the possibility to make choices, the European scholars Gaël Brulé and Ruut Veenhoven (2014) have described psychological freedom as the capacity to make life choices and the absence of inner restrictions. The young woman who decides to forego leaving her violent boyfriend because she cannot imagine herself alone exhibits the opposite of psychological freedom – that is to say, psychological unfreedom. In addition to possibility, the social conditions that make choosing possible, and the capacity and personal characteristics to make a choice, freedom therefore requires opportunity. Subjective freedom is, in other words, enabled or restricted by structural unfreedom. When we teach psychological freedom in African psychology classes, we have to take note of the conditions of freedom or unfreedom under which the students and their parents exist.

Like other psychologists, Mihaly Csikszentmihalyi and Ronald Graef (1980) reduce freedom to attributions concerning the voluntariness of our own or others' actions. They note that while it has often been held that the quality of human life is enhanced by freedom, freedom is a multidimensional phenomenon under which we can include philosophical, political, social and psychological dimensions. We consider quality of life, a life of well-being and meaning, a secure life, to be an imperative when living in an anti-black world in the aftermath of colonialism and apartheid. For those who wish to increase the well-being of African lives – as we do – measuring the contribution of psychological autonomy to the quality of African lives is a necessity. And for those of us who want to measure psychological freedom – as we do – the multidimensionality of freedom makes accurately defining it a vital task. African psychology is not to be confused with theoretical psychology or qualitative psychology. Methodological and technical development and sophistication are part of the terrain.

Burrhus Frederic Skinner (1971), the leading figure in behaviourism, famously argued that freedom is not a state of mind or feeling, as the philosophers and many psychologists would have it, but a result of the process of operant conditioning which is contingent upon consequences referred to as reinforcers. Operant conditioning occurs when behaviour is repeated because it is followed by certain reinforcements which may be positive (money) or negative (the reduction of controlling behaviour). A woman who succeeds in making her psychologically abusive husband stop maltreating her is likely to repeat the actions that made the abuse stop. A child achieves all As in her exams, the parents are pleased and buy her gifts, she strives for more As because this pleases the parents and the parents will buy her more gifts. An employer hires undocumented migrants because he pays them low wages, and when any worker asks for higher wages he fires her; most migrants never voice their disgruntlement, reinforcing the practice of only employing migrants and the employer's view that migrant workers are better employees than locals. This is not to agree with Skinner regarding whether or not freedom is all about contingencies of reinforcement, and that all humans can do is choose the type of control to which they submit, since they cannot escape control, but to further indicate the elusiveness of psychological freedom.

Barry Schwartz, an American psychologist who wrote an article in which he critiques rational-choice theory (Schwartz 2000), argues that too much self-determination is not freedom but self-defeating tyranny. Even though I am inclined towards its warning about too much choice, that argument betrays where it comes from: the heart of a culture which privileges individualism, where a multitude of toothpaste brands can be found on the supermarket shelves, and where everything appears to be available for purchase; that is to say, an American culture in which the market economy is godlike. Even in America, though, for those whose lives have been constrained by dehumanising laws, freedom is not to be taken for granted. Under slavery, there were not many positive choices available other than to fight for freedom. Under conditions of colonial rule, apartheid, racism and dictatorship, we have to keep teaching and learning freedom.

Psychological freedom, being such a historically inflected, dense, context-dependent phenomenon, is a founding supposition of African psychology. Racism does not end at the structural level – the level of the law, police, white terrorism, segregated neighbourhoods and unequal education – but requires psychological strategies to oppress, to govern, to terrorise, segregate and make unequal. Racist control is a behavioural, cognitive and emotional condition as much as a legal, institutional and representational fact. Hence, to free people's actions, thoughts, perceptions and feelings, we need a disciplinary orientation that is not reluctant to nurture African psychological self-determination.

Psychological freedom is vital because patriarchal sexist oppression is not only about laws concerning marriage, rape, reproductive health or equal pay for the same work. It is also located in motivation and practice and attitudes about who can and cannot marry, under what 'traditions', and the very meaning of marriage; in myths about the discourse of 'real rape' versus that which encourages victims not to make a big deal about what your boyfriend or husband did; in how society regards women who want abortions, the structures put in place and resources deployed to take care of unwanted pregnancy, or the lack of such structures and resources; in the economic and cultural price we put on what many have traditionally seen as women's work, such as food preparation or rearing children, and the policies and actions that exist to back or undercut that pricing.

Psychological freedom is imperative because economic exploitation is buttressed by institutional structures and cultures like discriminatory hiring and promotion practices, unfair policies and unequal pay, but also arises from and affects the contents of our minds and our emotional world.

As an undertaking intended to psychologically understand the world from here, African psychology also aims to liberate us from oppressive Euroamerican-centred psychology and to free psychology as a global endeavour from colonial-modern notions of being human in the world as it exists.

Psychological autonomy is about claiming for ourselves the right to look. To create. Be wrong. Question.

Freedom to design a new environment. Freedom to fail. Freedom to ask more questions.

Tolerance of the fact that others will, quite often, disagree with you, and that this is an absolutely acceptable fact.

The opportunity to relearn, having come from under a repressive regime, the inevitability and affective rewards of the equal freedom of others.

The ever-present possibility of receiving a 'no', that is to say, the response that you did not want – being fine with rejection. (Yet a 'yes' can also be an unfavourable response when the answer you were hoping for is 'no'.)

Psychological freedom means being free to ask uncomfortable questions in the face of pressure to keep quiet – not just questions for others, but precisely questions about the things we hold dear, such as whether God exists; whether Africans are inherently corrupt; whether, indeed, Africans are intellectually inferior to Asians or Europeans; whether women prefer men who are strong; or whether only the upper classes ought to have children.

When we psychologically experience our own humanity as inferior, when we believe that we are not entitled – a word I like – to be in the world as others are, no law can change our experience and belief.

When the self considers itself to be not as good as another, work on the self is the only cure.

It would seem that individuals who are mentally and emotionally free are more secure in their ability to create, be wrong, happily disagree with others, and deal with stomach failure. To question. To feel that the world belongs to all who live in it. To open themselves to the world, enabling them to listen, learn and grow, without feeling that they will be psychologically annihilated.

As a university teacher I have learned that the self-belief and ability to question received knowledge is one of the greatest gifts a teacher – or parent – can give their students and offspring. This gift that leads to true knowledge and confidence in your ideas, including knowledge of yourself, materialises out of having posed questions to yourself and to the world.

One Tuesday morning, while dropping my child at school, I saw a sign that read: 'ideas, ideas, ideas; many different ideas; share your ideas; be different'. It was not on that Tuesday morning that I learned of the fact that some schools, perhaps all modern schools, encourage children to have ideas. However, I was reminded of how much some of us take this for granted. Whatever ideas you the parent have, whatever your family traditions teach or your culture thinks about democracy in the school and at home – by which I mean a school or home where children are acknowledged to have questions and their own views – modern schools and universities value students who share their ideas, speak, give good presentations and ask questions. Hence, to teach African children to approach what they see, hear, read and learn from others, from television, Google, movies, Facebook, books, Twitter, newspapers, Snapchat, Instagram, WhatsApp, other social media, and even from their teachers – even from you the parent – with a questioning attitude sets those children up for success in such an educational system.

Now there have tended to be two groups that seem restrained from voicing their opinions and offering their responses in classes: female students and black students. Hence, black female students tend to be most restrained in voicing their views in class. It is particularly when these students lack the confidence to express themselves in the medium of instruction – which in many African universities is one of the colonial languages – that they attend an endless number of classes without ever saying a word. It is not always the case, but I suspect there are many students who must find school a terrifyingly joyless experience, not only an oppressive one. To mutely attend lecture after lecture, one semester after another, year in year out, without finding anything to trigger a contribution from you, cannot be a great way to pass the time.

More than our desires for them to succeed at school, to get a tertiary qualification and a high-paying job, to start a successful business of their own, we have to develop in black female and male children a feeling of and familiarity with freedom. This sense of freedom includes ecstatic scepticism about what they learn at school, in lecture rooms, and from parents, friends and the media. If we nurture in our students and children – to whom we will entrust Africa – free, secure and questioning psyches, they will be less likely to suspect us of oppressing them, were we committed to or unwittingly doing so. Only when they are free to be wrong, enabled to question the traditions and truths that make up their society, and also to question science, law, history, identity, indeed everything, will African children and young people find out what freedom in their lives can mean, what they can do with freedom, and therefore be able to give their considered and authentic responses to the questions they will inexorably have to answer.

99 | Think Africa in the world

This exercise has been an invitation to African-centred psychology. It is an invitation to those who are done with being alienated to contribute towards the development of an internationalist African-centred psychology. It is a call for a psychology that places Africans centre-stage in working out the meaning of their own lives. It is about knowing Africans, from psychologists and students of psychology to the many lay African publics, from a disalienated position, which is one of resisting, overcoming, or working through feelings and the sense of being unloved and misrecognised. It is a call for thinking about who you are, in relation to yourself and others. It is about learning about the world from within your own embodiedness and locatedness in the world, and so achieving what we can call a sense of relatedness.

African-centred psychology is, centrally, about experiencing the self and the world from a place in Africa. This place is not one place. But whatever home is for you, that is the place from which you go out into the world.

African-centred psychology is an emancipatory psychology that aims to help students, researchers, therapists and activists, within as well as outside Africa, to engender a stronger position for psychological insights from Africa.

This, then, has been a call inspired by the space that has reopened in several places on the continent to *make* African-centred psychological thought and practice. A call that sees an opportunity for radical, critical, anarchist and social-justice-oriented psychologists from Africa and other parts of the world to contribute towards their own demarginalisation and disalienation. A call to break free from the conceptual prison created by psychology coming from the US and Western Europe – a psychology that we ourselves have supported. A call to contribute to thinking Africa in the world.

100 | Always the future

I will not have the final word. Especially when we consider the future, such as what an introductory textbook on African-centred psychology would look like – or one on social African psychology, or on neuropsychology from an African-centred perspective, or on African-centred child development, or on any other area of psychology that situates African realities, African-centred knowledge and knowledge-making, and African lives at the centre – it is obvious that a great many more words have to come, a great deal more work is necessary.

However, in the end I return to the questions that contain the most potential for the work that must be done towards centring Africa in psychology. What does it mean to say African in African psychology is tacit? What precisely does the project of centring Africa and Africans entail? When will the time come when the majority of African students of psychology and African psychologists have overcome the enervating, even retraumatising, inferiority complexes imposed on them in relation to US and European psychology?

To say that African in African psychology should be tacit means we need to constantly remind ourselves that the world makes most sense from our own perspectives – unless we are asked, not compelled or consciously wish, to adopt the Other's perspective. I say it again to remind myself: African in African psychology is silent.

Achieving this involves conscientising yourself towards a place where you feel entitled to your body, your voice, your affective and cognitive life, your perspective. If you have ever felt that your views do not matter, now is a good day to start learning to trust what you see and feel and think.

The project of centring Africa and Africans entails learning to read any psychology text, test or tool as a thing from *somewhere*. There are no value-neutral textbooks. There is no study or theory that does not assume certain beliefs about the self, others and the world. You cannot, then, read anything well if you read it as from *nowhere*. This is what Euroamerican psychology has managed to make us forget – that it comes mainly from Western Europe and the US. All knowledge is from somewhere, made by people under specific circumstances, provoked by certain problems that exist around them. And it is only from somewhere that you can read things from somewhere.

The time when we will be totally happy, it is true, is always the future. That is no cause for despair. It implies that we can never stand still, until we arrive in that future.

As a teacher, having educated yourself to appreciate all psychology as a way to think of the world from a certain place, as made by some people from somewhere, the next step is to learn to teach your students how to read the world from a place in Africa, how to undertake Africa-centring research in Africa primarily but not only for Africa, how to help to address the psychological health of Africans and non-Africans with the tools developed here.

African-centred psychological work entails psychologists and students having to learn to refuse imposed *double names*. That is why I came to be known also as Robert, my father Moses Nteke, my mother Gloria Mathabiso. To note double names is to reference something that is all too familiar and deeply poignant for many people in countries where colonising powers were supported by Christian missionaries, which means most former colonies. Under the colonial Christian missions the colonised were forced to have so-called 'pronounceable' or Christian names – which in Africa happened to be Dutch, English, French, or Portuguese names – in addition to, or as replacements for, their 'heathen' or indigenous names. The practice of renaming new initiates is also common in Islam. It is for this reason (though it is not the only one) that we encounter names like Jacob Gedleyihlekisa Zuma, the fourth president of South Africa. In *Long Walk to Freedom*, Rolihlahla Mandela speaks about how he got the name Nelson (Mandela 1994). It is a funny story. But it is terrifically distressing, too, that the colonised were coerced by white patriarchal Christian colonial supremacy to favour the names it brought with it, to name themselves using its lexicon, to say its names. We must, then, reject imposed double names. We must be psychologists, or we can never fully be ourselves for ourselves. You are a neuropsychologist, that's it. Given the sub-specialities, you are a particular kind of psychologist, of course. In that case, you must be an (African) social psychologist, period. You are a clinical (African) psychologist, that's it. You must be an educational (African) psychologist, nothing less and nothing more. But, then, although you have to refuse a double name – African psychologist – or triple names like African social psychologist, African clinical psychologist, or African feminist psychologist, you have to find supple ways, as you travel with others (non-African fellow travellers in psychology), to remain faithful to Africa as the centre of your perspective.

And yet – this is key – Africa (not North America, not Western Europe) must always be the unspoken term, the centre, the originating ground and standard for the fitness of our theories, research, activities, praxis. Otherwise we have a very strange sort of social science that is clueless about society.

We have a psychology that has little idea of what shapes or deforms the psyches of the people living here. Africa must be at the centre. That's it.

Although I make it sound like a walk in the park, it is a hard task to accomplish.

References

Adhikari, M. (2008) '"Streams of blood and streams of money": New perspectives on the annihilation of the Herero and Nama peoples of Namibia, 1904–1908'. *Kronos* 34(1): 303–320.

Ahluwalia, P. (2003) 'Fanon's nausea: The hegemony of the white nation'. *Social Identities: Journal for the Study of Race, Nation and Culture* 9: 341–356.

Ahmed, S. (2017) *Living a Feminist Life*. Durham, NC & London: Duke University Press.

Akbar, N.I. (1984) 'Africentric social sciences for human liberation'. *Journal of Black Studies* 14(4): 395–414.

Asante, M.K. (1991) 'The Afrocentric idea in education'. *The Journal of Negro Education* 60(2): 170–180.

Asante, M.K. (2007) *An Afrocentric Manifesto: Toward an African Renaissance*. Cambridge: Polity Press.

Asante, M.K. & Mazama, A. (2005) *Encyclopedia of Black Studies*. London: Sage.

Baldwin, J.A. (1986) 'African (Black) psychology: Issues and synthesis'. *Journal of Black Studies* 16(3): 235–249.

Berger, J. (1972) *Ways of Seeing*. London: British Broadcasting Corporation & Penguin Books.

Biko, S. (1987) *I Write What I Like: Steve Biko. A Selection of His Writings*, edited by A. Stubbs. Oxford: Heinemann.

Bishop, J.P., Sonn, C.C., Fisher, A.T. & Drew, N.M. (2001) 'Community-based community psychology: Perspectives from Australia'.

In Seedat, M. (ed.) *Community Psychology: Theory, Method, and Practice*. Cape Town: Oxford University Press.

Brown, L. (1993) *The New Shorter Oxford English Dictionary on Historical Principles*. Oxford: Clarendon Press.

Brulé, G. & Veenhoven, R. (2014) 'Freedom and happiness in nations: Why the Finns are happier than the French'. *Psychology of Well-Being: Theory, Research and Practice* 4(17). http://www.psywb.com/content/4/1/17 (accessed April 2019).

Bulhan, H.A. (1980) 'Psychological research in Africa: Genesis and function'. *Présence Africaine (Nouvelle serie)* 116(4e Trimestre): 20–42.

Césaire, A. (1972) *Discourse on Colonialism*, translated by J. Pinkham. New York: Monthly Review Press.

Clark, K. (1955) *Prejudice and Your Child*. Boston: Beacon Press.

Clark, K.B. & Clark, M.P. (1939a) 'The development of consciousness of self and the emergence of racial identification in Negro preschool children'. *Journal of Social Psychology* 10: 591–599.

Clark, K.B. & Clark, M.P. (1939b) 'Segregation as a factor in the racial identification of Negro preschool children'. *Journal of Experimental Education* 11: 161–163.

Clark, K.B. & Clark, M.P. (1940) 'Skin color as a factor in racial identification of Negro preschool children'. *Journal of Social Psychology* 11: 159–169.

Clark, K.B. & Clark, M.P. (1950) 'Emotional factors in racial identification and preference in Negro children'. *Journal of Negro Education* 19(3) (*The Negro Child in the American Social Order*): 341–350.

Cokley, K., Awosogba, P. & Taylor, D. (2013) 'A 12-year content analysis of the *Journal of Black Psychology* (2000–2011): Implications for the field of black psychology'. *Journal of Black Psychology* 40(3): 215–238.

Cooper, S. (2013) 'Africanizing South African psychology'. *Journal of Black Psychology* 39(3): 212–222.

Couve, C. (1986) 'Psychology and politics in Manganyi's work: A materialist critique'. *Psychology in Society* 5: 90–130.

Cross, W.E. (1978) 'The Thomas and Cross models of psychological nigrescence: A review'. *Journal of Black Psychology* 5(1): 13–31.

Cross, W.E. (2009) 'Foreword'. In Neville, H.A., Tynes, B.M. & Utsey, S.O. (eds) *Handbook of African American Psychology*. London: Sage.

Csikszentmihalyi, M. & Graef, R. (1980) 'The experience of freedom in daily life'. *American Journal of Community Psychology* 8(4): 401–414.

Fanon, F. (1963) *The Wretched of the Earth*, translated by C. Farrington. New York: Grove Press.

Fanon, F. (1967) *Toward the African Revolution: Political Essays*, translated by H. Chevalier. New York: Grove Press.

Fanon, F. (1970) *Black Skin, White Masks*, translated by C.L. Markmann. London: Paladin.

Freire, P. (2005) *Pedagogy of the Oppressed*, translated by M. Bergman Ramos. New York: Continuum.

Garuba, H. (2012) 'African studies, area studies, and the logic of the disciplines'. In Nhlapo, T. & Garuba, H. (eds) *African Studies in the Post-colonial University*. Rondebosch: University of Cape Town/ Centre for African Studies.

Gewald, J.-B. (2003) 'Herero genocide in the twentieth century: Politics and memory'. In Abbink, J., De Bruijn, M. & Walraven, K. (eds) *Rethinking Resistance: Revolt and Violence in African History*. Leiden & Boston: Brill.

Gimlin, D. (2013) '"Too good to be real": The obviously augmented breast in women's narratives of cosmetic surgery'. *Gender & Society* 27(6): 913–934.

Gordon, L.R. (2007) 'Problematic people and epistemic decoloni-zation: Toward the postcolonial in Africana political thought'. In Persram, N. (ed.) *Postcolonialism and Political Theory*. Lanham, MD: Lexington Books.

Hook, D. (2005) 'A critical psychology of the postcolonial'. *Theory and Psychology* 15(4): 475–503.

Hountondji, P.J. (1987) 'On the universality of science and technology'. In Lutz, B. & Deutsche Gesellschaft für Soziologie (DGS) (eds) *Technik und Sozialer Wandel: Verhandlungen des 23. Deutschen Soziologentages in Hamburg 1986*. Frankfurt am Main: Campus Verlag.

Hountondji, P. (1990) 'Scientific dependence in Africa today'. *Research in African Literatures* 21(3): 5–15.

Huysamen, M. (2017) 'A critical analysis of men's constructions of paying for sex: Doing gender, doing race in the interview context'. PhD thesis, Department of Psychology, University of Cape Town.

Jackson, G.G. (1982) 'Black psychology: An avenue to the study of Afro-Americans'. *Journal of Black Studies* 12(3): 241–260.

Johnson, R.W. (2014) 'Mamphela Ramphele: The DA decides to blow itself up'. *Politicsweb* 30 January. http://www.politicsweb.co.za/politicsweb/view/politicsweb/en/page71619?oid=526657&sn=Detail&pid=71616 (accessed February 2014).

Karenga, M. (1988) 'Black Studies and the problematic of paradigm: The philosophical dimension'. *Journal of Black Studies* 18(4): 395–414.

Long, W. (2016) 'On the Africanization of psychology'. *South African Journal of Psychology* 46(4): 429–431.

Mandela, R.N. (1994) *Long Walk to Freedom*. London: Abacus.

Manganyi, N.C. (1970) 'Neurotic compromise solutions and symptom sophistication in cases of hysteria'. *South African Medical Journal* 23 May: 607–609.

Manganyi, N.C. (1973) *Being-Black-in-the-World*. Johannesburg: Spro-cas/Ravan Press.

Manganyi, N.C. (1977a) *Alienation and the Body in Racist Society: A Study of the Society that Invented Soweto*. New York: NOK Publishers.

Manganyi, N.C. (1977b) *Mashangu's Reverie, and Other Essays*. Johannesburg: Ravan Press.

Manganyi, N.C. (1981) *Looking through the Keyhole: Dissenting Essays on the Black Experience*. Johannesburg: Ravan Press.

Manganyi, N.C. (1991) *Treachery and Innocence: Psychology and Racial Difference in South Africa*. Johannesburg: Ravan Press.

Manganyi, N.C. (2013) 'On becoming a psychologist in apartheid South Africa'. *South African Journal of Psychology* 43(3): 278–288.

Marable, M. (ed.) (2000) *Dispatches from the Ebony Tower: Intellectuals Confront the African American Experience*. New York: Columbia University Press.

Maunier, R. (1949) *The Sociology of Colonies: An Introduction to the Study of Race Contact* (Volume 1). London: Routledge & Kegan Paul.

Mbembe, A. (2001) *On the Postcolony*. Berkeley and Los Angeles: University of California Press.

Mbembe, A. (2003) 'Necropolitics'. *Public Culture* 15(1): 11–40.

McKaiser, E. (2014) 'Why does RW Johnson think blacks associate white leadership with excellence?' *POWERFM987* 5 February.

http://www.powerfm.co.za/podcasts/why-does-rw-johnson-think-blacks-associate-white-leadership-with-excellence/ (accessed February 2014).

Melber, H. (2005) 'How to come to terms with the past: Re-visiting the German colonial genocide in Namibia'. *Afrika Spectrum* 40(1): 139–148.

Mignolo, W.D. (2005) 'Prophets facing sidewise: The geopolitics of knowledge and the colonial difference'. *Social Epistemology* 19(1): 111–127.

Mignolo, W. (2010) 'Cosmopolitanism and the de-colonial option'. *Studies in Philosophy and Education* 29(2): 111–127.

Mkhize, N. (2004) 'Psychology: An African perspective'. In Ratele, K., Duncan, N., Hook, D., Kiguwa, P., Mkhize, N. & Collins, A. (eds) *Self, Psychology and Community*. Lansdowne: UCT Press.

Ndlovu-Gatsheni, S.J. (2013) *Coloniality of Power in Postcolonial Africa: Myths of Decolonization*. Dakar: Council for the Development of Social Science Research in Africa.

Nicholas, L. (2003a) 'Introduction to psychology'. In Nicholas, L. (ed.) *Introduction to Psychology*. Lansdowne: UCT Press.

Nicholas, L. (ed.) (2003b) *Introduction to Psychology*. Lansdowne: UCT Press.

Nicholas, L. (2014) 'A history of South African (SA) psychology'. *Universitas Psychologica* 13(5): 1983–1991.

Nobles, W.W. (1991) 'African philosophy: Foundations for black psychology'. In Jones, R.L. (ed.) *Black Psychology*. Berkeley, CA: Cobb & Henry Publishers.

Nobles, W.W. (2013) 'Fundamental task and challenge of black psychology'. *Journal of Black Psychology* 39(3): 292–299.

Nobles, W.W. (2015) 'From black psychology to *Sakhu Djaer*: Implications for the further development of a Pan African Black psychology'. *Journal of Black Psychology* 41(5): 399–414.

Nsamenang, A.B. (1995) 'Factors influencing the development of psychology in Sub-Saharan Africa'. *International Journal of Psychology* 30(6): 729–739.

Nwoye, A. (2015) 'What is African psychology the psychology of?' *Theory and Psychology* 25(1): 96–116.

Nwoye, A. (2017) 'An Africentric theory of human personhood'. *Psychology in Society* 54: 42–66.

Olukoshi, A. (2012) 'Re-making African studies in the post-colonial Africa university: Some notes'. In Nhlapo, T. & Garuba, H. (eds) *African Studies in the Post-colonial University*. Rondebosch: University of Cape Town/Centre for African Studies.

Painter, D., Kiguwa, P. & Böhmke, W. (2013) 'Contexts and continuities of critique: Reflections on the current state of critical psychology in South Africa'. *Annual Review of Critical Psychology* 13: 849–869.

Parham, T.A. (1989) 'Cycles of psychological nigrescence'. *The Counseling Psychologist* 17(2): 187–226.

Parker, I. (2007) *Revolution in Psychology: Alienation to Emancipation*. London: Pluto Press.

Psychology in Society (2016) *Call for Papers for a PINS Special Issue: African Psychologies for the World*. Durban: Psychology in Society.

Ratele, K. (2017a) 'Four (African) psychologies'. *Theory and Psychology* 27(3): 313–327.

Ratele, K. (2017b) 'Six theses on African psychology for the world'. *Psychology in Society* 54: 1–9.

Ratele, K., Cornel, C., Dlamini, S., Helman, R., Malherbe, N. & Titi, N. (2018) 'Some basic questions about (a) decolonizing African-centred psychology considered'. *South African Journal of Psychology* 48(3): 331–342.

Rhodes University (2019) *Social Change: Psychology and the Social Change Award*. https://www.ru.ac.za/psychology/socialchange/ (accessed April 2019).

Rojas, F. (2007) *From Black Power to Black Studies: How a Radical Social Movement Became an Academic Discipline*. Baltimore, MD: Johns Hopkins University Press.

Santrock, J.W. (2000) *Psychology* (6th edition). Boston: McGraw-Hill.

Schwartz, B. (2000) 'Self-determination: The tyranny of freedom'. *American Psychologist* 55(1): 79–88.

Seedat, M. (2001) *Community Psychology: Theory, Method, and Practice*. Cape Town: Oxford University Press.

Semenya, B. & Mokwena, M. (2012) 'African cosmology, psychology and community'. In Visser, M. & Moleko, A. (eds) *Community Psychology in South Africa* (2nd edition). Pretoria: Van Schaik.

Skinner, B.F. (1971) *Beyond Freedom and Dignity*. Harmondsworth: Penguin Books.

Smuts, J.C. (1973) *Walt Whitman: A Study in the Evolution of Personality.* Detroit, MI: Wayne State University Press.

Sparks, E. (2001) 'Community mental health in the USA: Challenges to urban community mental health centres'. In Seedat, M. (ed.) *Community Psychology: Theory, Method, and Practice.* Cape Town: Oxford University Press.

Triandis, H.C. (1994) *Culture and Social Behaviour.* New York: McGraw-Hill.

Visser, M. & Moleko, A. (eds) (2012) *Community Psychology in South Africa* (2nd edition). Pretoria: Van Schaik.

Wa Thiong'o, N. (1986) *Decolonising the Mind: The Politics of Language in African Literature.* London: James Currey.

Wa Thiong'o, N. (1993) *Moving the Centre: The Struggle for Cultural Freedoms.* London: James Currey.

Wilcocks, R.W. (1917) 'Zur Erkenntnistheorie Hegels in der Phäno-menologie des Geistes'. PhD thesis, Friedrich-Wilhelms-Universität, Berlin.

Index

Printed and bound by CPI Group (UK) Ltd, Croydon, CR0 4YY

09/06/2025

14685813-0002